To Re-Enchant the World

A Philosophy of
Unitarian Universalism

Richard Grigg

To order additional copies of this book, contact:
Xlibris Corporation
1-888-795-4274
www.Xlibris.com
Orders@Xlibris.com

26103

Contents

TO MY FELLOW SEEKERS IN
THE UNITARIAN SOCIETY OF NEW HAVEN

Introduction

The Sea of Faith
Was once, too, at the full, and round earth's shore
Lay like the folds of a bright girdle furled.
But now I only hear
Its melancholy, long, withdrawing roar . . . .
— Matthew Arnold, "Dover Beach"[1]

You thinkers, prisoners of what will work:
a dog ran by me in the street one night,
its path met by its feet in quick unthought,
and I stopped in a sudden Christmas, purposeless,
a miracle without a proof, soon lost.

But I still call, 'Here, Other, Other,' in the dark.
— William Stafford, "An Epiphany"[2]

Most observers of Western culture claim that, beginning as early as the seventeenth century, we have been living in an increasingly secular world, a world, in other words, in which religion and spirituality have a much smaller role to play than they did in the pre-modern era. It cannot be put better than the great sociologist Max Weber put it: modern economies, with their highly rational rules for how society should be structured, have "disenchanted" the world.[3] They have removed a sense of the sacred, the Holy, the Mysterious. The Sea of Faith had already receded in the nineteenth century to such a degree

9

that the famous German philosopher Friedrich Nietzsche could make his epochal proclamation that God is dead. And in the twentieth-century, Jewish theologian Martin Buber, thinking especially of the implications of the Nazi Holocaust, spoke poignantly about the "eclipse of God," about God withdrawing his face from us.[4]

This process of secularization and disenchantment was not so much the result of a self-conscious attempt to eradicate religion—though there were some, such as Karl Marx and Sigmund Freud, who did wish to see religion disappear—as of impersonal forces unleashed by modernization. Even Universalism and Unitarianism might be read as having been unwittingly caught up in this process! The early American Unitarians and Universalists were, needless to say, pious Christians. But both groups freed themselves from what they regarded as the constraints and dogmatism of more traditional Christianity. As Unitarianism and Universalism developed in this country, their members maintained the strongest of suspicions about obligatory creeds and doctrines. As a result, Universalism and Unitarianism became homes for religious skeptics. As Unitarian Universalist minister Kathleen McTigue has observed, if we were to select a U.U. patron saint, our first inclination might be to choose "doubting Thomas" of New Testament fame.[5] Now skepticism is, on the one hand, a proud and important part of our U.U. heritage. It is kept alive thanks, in large part, to the all-important contribution of U.U. humanism. But if skepticism is allowed to stand in stark isolation from all of our other human sensibilities, it might indeed become one culprit in the disenchantment of the world.

Secularization and disenchantment are readily evident in Europe, where churches and temples are often nearly empty. As Niall Ferguson reports, regarding the Christian tradition in particular, "In the Netherlands, Britain, Germany, Sweden and Denmark today, fewer than 1 in 10 people now attend church once a month or more. Some 52 percent of Norwegians and 55 percent of Swedes say that God did [sic] not matter to them at all.''[6] Even in Japan, despite its different cultural roots, religious observance has fallen off sharply among younger people.

The United States may seem an exception to the process of secularization. After all, Americans still appear to be a church-going people, and religious references permeate even our political discourse. Why is America different? Of course, this country was founded by persons seeking to escape religious persecution, so that religion had a unique role in the origins of the United States of America. But surely the forces of the industrial and post-industrial ages should have washed away this peculiarity of our Colonial beginnings by now. The solution to the puzzle is to be found, aver many sociologists of American religion, in the fact that other countries have, or had, government-established churches, from Shinto in Japan to Anglicanism and Lutheranism in Europe. Where religion simply comes along with one's cultural baggage, it can easily become an unthinking and ultimately unimportant part of one's life. But America's religious pluralism means that religions have always had to compete with one another, to aggressively market themselves. Thus, just as Wheaties cereal has long been the "Breakfast of Champions," Unitarian Universalism is now the "Uncommon Denomination." This never-ending advertising campaign has apparently kept religion alive in America.

Yet, American piety is not quite as vibrant as it appears on the surface. There is a devastating shortage of priests in the Roman Catholic Church; Catholic parishes and Church-run schools are not infrequently being shut down; and the Catholic Church is presently being torn by disclosures of sexual abuse by clergy. Judaism is losing many of its children to intermarriage. So-called "mainline Protestantism" has been shedding members for decades. As is so often observed, it is evangelical or fundamentalist Christianity that is growing. But one requires very little imagination to see that fundamentalism is itself a child of secularization, a religious retreat behind walls of denial intended to shield one from the forces of modernity and postmodernity.[7]

Of course some theorists reject, or at least modify, the "secularization hypothesis" by saying that religion and spirituality, rather than simply disappearing, are taking on new forms. The most useful example in the United States is provided by the host of New Age pieties that have sprung up in the last forty years. It only takes a quick trip to the religion section of a local bookstore or a perusal of the Internet to see that New Age spirituality is indeed exploding in popularity. But if New Age and other more personal, less institutional, pieties represent spirituality in an altered form, this is nonetheless a fragmented and more inchoate spirituality than the one that informed the America of old. Rituals that I perform alone in my living room, or even with a dozen co-religionists, probably cannot manifest the sacred in quite the powerful fashion that the old-time religion could. In the former case, I do not have the presence of a sufficient number of other persons to imbue my spiritual commitments with a sense of objectivity and reality. After all, what makes my interpretation of the world seem real to me is precisely the phenomenon of inter-subjectivity: my interpretation is confirmed by those around me. Hence the stories about anthropologists living in cultural worlds different from their own in order to study these "strange" ways of seeing reality, only to "go native," in other words, to buy into the world of those being studied: the world *is* as I see it reflected by those among whom I live. If my worldview is too idiosyncratic, then I am left without a social "plausibility structure."[8] The old-time religion may be giving way to a host of new pieties, but too many of these new and radical pieties fail to attain the critical mass of membership required to build a robust social plausibility structure. Unfortunately, pockets of questers sprinkled here and there throughout our society, each with a different spiritual agenda, cannot succeed in re-enchanting the world.

Of course, if these diverse new pieties, along with the bits and pieces of the more traditional religious faiths that still haunt our consciousness, could somehow be brought together into a single community where they were practiced face-to-face with other persons, then perhaps the needed critical mass could be attained, and the sacred would indeed be rejuvenated. Spirituality could then be just as potent a force as it was in previous centuries. And this possibility brings us to the central claim of this book, namely, *that contemporary Unitarian Universalism, with its unique ability to bring together a plethora of different spiritualities within a single community, is a particularly powerful site for the re-enchantment of the world, for the rebirth of the sacred.* Unitarian Universalism is about identity-in-difference: the spiritual quest must, given our contemporary emphasis on the integrity of the individual, always be one's "ownmost" undertaking, but one makes the spiritual journey in community, alongside a host of others on their own unique quests.[9] We are on a solitary journey together, and it is through this mix of pluralism and unity that the sacred is reborn. Of course this is indeed a *re*-birth: the sacred that appears is as potent as that which revealed itself in the past, before Matthew Arnold's Sea of Faith began to recede, but it also reveals itself in a different manner.

The rebirth of sacrality is midwifed by what can logically be designated the second half of U.U. history. The first half (thinking simply in terms of America) began in the late eighteenth century. For instance, John Murray came to America in 1777 and began preaching universalism; and King's Chapel in Boston, an Anglican church, revised its Book of Common Prayer in 1785 to reflect unitarian sensibilities.[10] This first half of U.U. history ends in 1960. In 1961, the second half of our history begins, with the uniting of Unitarianism and Universalism in the Unitarian Universalist Association. But this way of halving our history is not simply a function of the fact that the U.U.A. was formed in 1961. Rather, it is also the case that the 1960s and the following decades enhanced U.U. pluralism to a crucial degree, so that it could incorporate—literally "embody"—a whole host of different spiritualities. It was in these years, after all, that U.U.s really began to embrace Asian spiritualities, eco-spirituality, and feminism, to name but a few of the most important new movements. Thus, the 1985 General Assembly finalized the U.U. Principles and Sources, which emphasize the dignity of *all* persons and encourage us to draw upon not only Judaism and Christianity in building our spiritualities, but also on the wisdom of other world religions. And in 1995, the General Assembly added to the list of our spiritual sources the "Spiritual teachings of Earth-centered traditions which celebrate the sacred circle of life and instruct us to live in harmony with the rhythms of nature."[11]

It shall be our task in Chapter One to define a particular model of spirituality. This is a crucial, if preliminary, step. For one thing, "spirituality" is often a "weasel word."[12] That is, it is the sort of word that we sometimes throw around without ever being precise about what we intend it to mean, so that it ends up being vacuous, having no significant meaning at all. But, more important, we need to be able to show that there can be a common denominator, a formal unity even when there is no unity of content, to diverse forms of spirituality so that we can discern an identity-in-difference among spiritual paths. For if there is no such underlying unity, then the attempt to bring together a host of different spiritualities within a single community in order to give all of them social plausibility will result not in the rebirth of sacrality, but rather in a literally unbearable chaos, so that any institution attempting to shoulder this pluralism will simply collapse onto the ground. Think too about the fact that if there be no underlying structural unity to our diverse spiritual quests, then we cannot all find sustenance in a single, Sunday-morning gathering.

The rebirth of the sacred that I have in mind, then, is by no means simply a matter of the appearance of many new and diverse spiritual paths in American piety. Instead, it is the result of a particular chemistry among these paths, an underlying bond that allows the sacred to emerge. It is a product of that particular unity-in-difference found in Unitarian Universalist communities. This is certainly not intended to be what theologians call a "triumphalist" claim, that is, a claim that one's own religious group is superior to all others. Perhaps the sacred is being reborn in many places in our contemporary world. But I do want to go so far as to propose that the Unitarian Universalist community is playing an especially important and unique role in this rebirth. For one thing, it is only the member of a liberal religious community who will be willing to allow in the door a host of spiritualities decidedly different from her own. Some underlying, formal unity among spiritualties is not enough; one must be open to, even enthusiastic about, including them within one's own spiritual community. Put more precisely, an underlying structural unity among different spiritualities is a *necessary* but not a *sufficient* condition for re-enchanting the world. In addition to the underlying formal unity of different spiritual ways, one must have a liberal religious community that is willing to take advantage of that underlying unity and happily embrace all of these spiritual ways that, on the level of *content* in contrast to underlying structure, are radically diverse. The model of spirituality outlined in Chapter One will show how the unity-in-difference through which Unitarian Universalism re-enchants the world can be envisaged. It will be our stepping-stone to Chapter Two, where we shall zero in on a more particularly Unitarian Universalist spiritual pluralism.

Chapter Two will proceed by considering five familiar and diverse foci of U.U. piety: humanism, nature, the arts, social justice, and an empowering Source/Abyss of existence. Here we shall have the opportunity to be specific about the identity-in-difference of Unitarian Universalist beliefs. What is more, we shall end Chapter Two with the claim that the juxtaposition of so many different spiritual ways within his or her own community confronts the religious quester with a glimpse of what we shall call the Mysterious Depth of reality. This will not be a scientific mystery, something that would contradict the U.U. emphasis on the power and importance of reason, but rather an existential mystery, in other words a mystery that has to do with the fundamental questions about who we are, what our lives mean, and how we ought to live.

In Chapter Three, we shall attempt to understand, however inadequately, the sacred as it shows itself to us within the U.U.

community, the Other in the night that we continually seek and that sometimes deigns to appear. It is here that the potentially surprising claim will be set forth that Unitarian Universalism is, in its own unique way, a "sacramental" community. We shall explore the community's experience of the sacred in the Flower Communion, as well as in multi-dimensional sacred space, multi-faceted sacred time, and multi-vocative sacred language.

Chapter Four is a "Contrarian Interlude." It poses, and then attempts to refute, some of the major objections that might be aimed at the argument of this book. As an interlude, and a rather technical and fussy one at that, it may be the sort of writing that pious folks of old would say "does not tend toward edification." Readers who are not fond of philosophical nitpicking can easily skip Chapter Four, then, without losing the thread of the argument.

Chapter Five asks "Why Are We Here?" But it is not concerned with how the human species came to exist upon the earth but, rather, with why we U.U.s are here! In other words, what is the particular role of the Unitarian Universalist faith in the larger society, especially insofar as, according to my claim, Unitarian Universalism is a source for re-enchanting the world?

Finally, in Chapter Six we shall explore the notion of "divining" the future. This brief exploration will proffer some guesses about the future of Unitarian Universalism and raise the potentially touchy issue of U.U. proselytizing.

While the major goal of this book is to argue for the rebirth of sacrality via the particular way of being that we call Unitarian Universalism, it has another purpose as well: while contemporary Unitarian Universalism is *internally* pluralistic, there have been few books on Unitarian Universalism that grapple seriously with the numerous and exciting intellectual perspectives advanced by philosophers and other theorists in contemporary society. Given that U.U.s have always prided themselves on the intellectual integrity of their faith, this is a serious oversight. Other denominations, after all, boast theologians who continue to write books that put their particular faiths in dialogue with the most potent intellectual currents of our day, from quantum mechanics to postmodern theory. Perhaps such a dialogue is more difficult for U.U.s. After all, we have always rejected constraining creeds and authoritative theological pronouncements. But intellectual inquiry certainly need not be dogmatic, and any instance of human endeavor that loses the ability to bring the best resources of the culture to bear in intellectually rigorous self-scrutiny is destined to be thrown upon the scrap heap of history. I hope that the discussion that follows does at least a modest job of connecting the identity-in-difference of U.U. spirituality with wider intellectual perspectives in our culture.

I have subtitled this book "A Philosophy of Unitarian Universalism." What, then, is a philosophy of Unitarian Universalism? I take it to be an intellectual exploration of our faith that investigates that which makes it what it is, that gives it its peculiar identity. But rather than supposing that there exists some definitive list of U.U. characteristics, I am taking a more modest, and I hope more productive, tack: I am exploring one characteristic—the U.U. ability to re-enchant the world— that I believe is both crucial to U.U. identity and unique to it. Now any philosophy of Unitarian Universalism will, it seems to me, have to be, given the very nature of our community, a philosophy of U.U. *pluralism*. This is why a philosophy of Unitarian Universalism will never offer a definition of the U.U. tradition that can tie that tradition down via brittle, inflexible, dogmatic pronouncements. What is more, even philosophies of U.U. pluralism will themselves be pluralistic! That is, my own philosophy will be only one take on U.U. pluralism. But given the animating sensibilities of our community, that is as it should be. Let a thousand flowers bloom.

Notes for Introduction

[1] Matthew Arnold, "Dover Beach," in *The Norton Anthology of Poetry*, Shorter Edition, ed. Arthur M. Eastman et al. (New York: Norton, 1970), p. 396.

2   William Stafford, "An Epiphany," in William Stafford, *Stories That Could Be True: New And Collected Poems* (New York: Harper and Row, 1977), p. 182.

3   See Peter L. Berger on Weber in *The Sacred Canopy: Elements of a Sociological Theory of Religion* (Garden City, NY: Doubleday/ Anchor Books, 1967), p. 111.

4   See Eugene Borowitz's insightful treatment of Buber in Borowitz's *Choices in Modern Jewish Thought: A Partisan Guide* (New York: Behrman House, 1983).

5   The Reverend Kathleen McTigue, "Doubting Thomas as Patron Saint," a sermon preached at the Unitarian Society of New Haven (Connecticut), March 28, 2004.

6   Niall Ferguson, "Eurabia?" in *The New York Times Magazine*, April 4, 2004, p. 14.

7   A brief discussion of the notion of the postmodern will be offered in Chapter Two in our examination of humanism.

8   See Peter Berger, *The Sacred Canopy.*

9   The term "ownmost" is a translation of one of German philosopher Martin Heidegger's many neologisms. See Martin Heidegger, *Being and Time*, trans. John Macquarrie and Edward Robinson (New York: Harper and Row, 1962).

10   I employ the lower case here in talking about unitarianism and universalism because at this point they were not yet established institutions, but only particular religious perspectives.

11   The U.U. Principles and Sources can be found in the U.U. hymnbook, *Singing the Living Tradition* (Boston: Unitarian Universalist Association, 1993), p. x.

12   I borrow this apt little phrase from long-time Union Theological Seminary theologian Tom Driver.

Chapter One

Of the Empty Bowl, the Full Chalice, and the Hundred-Sided Polygon

The provocative Taoist masters make a great deal of the metaphor of the empty bowl. When we look at a bowl, we immediately suppose that what makes it what it is, what is really important about the bowl, is its shape, its material, and its general exterior details. But the Taoist sages ask us to consider the empty space inside the bowl. This emptiness, they point out, is what really matters. Without the emptiness, the bowl would be useless; it would not do its job as a bowl.

In our own lives, we ought to seek an emptiness akin to the bowl's. Ordinarily, we do the opposite. We allow our little egos to run our lives, scurrying about attempting to accomplish this and that. But this puts us and our egotistical desires on a collision course with what is, with nature and the realities of existence. Hence we are unhappy. Suppose that I want to go hiking Saturday morning, but I wake up, peer out the window, and see that the clouds are drenching the world with rain. My egotistical tendency will be to shout my anger and wave my fist at the meteorologist whose image on the television screen Friday night assured me that Saturday would bring sunshine. But this attitude only causes me to suffer. Much better to accept the fact that what is, simply is.

Emptiness enters this equation in the following fashion: I should empty myself of egotism, and allow the Tao, the infinite power that infuses the universe, to empower my attitudes and actions. I should, as the saying goes, "flow with the Tao." We confront the philosophy of *wu-wei* here, which introduces us to a *productive emptiness*. The revered scholar of world religions Huston Smith translates *wu-wei* as "creative quietude."[1] My ego is quiet. I have taken it off-line, as we might choose to put it today. The Tao takes the ego's place and creatively flows through me. Now I no longer resist nature and what is. Furthermore, once I am in harmony with the Tao, I need not worry about the goodness of my actions. We ought to follow Heaven and earth and "do nothing," says Chuang Tzu, "and [then] there is nothing that is not done."[2] In other words, the finite ego does nothing, but the Tao flowing through me leads me to right actions.[3] Emptiness is productive.

But now it is time to confess to the old "bait and switch" tactic: at this point in our discussion at least, my interest in the image of the empty bowl really lies elsewhere. Let us move from the sublime to the ridiculous, from the Taoist texts of ancient China to turn-of-the-century America's paradigmatic dysfunctional family, *The Simpsons*. There is one episode of that all-too-perceptive series in which a scene unfolds roughly as follows: it is the annual church picnic, and Reverend Lovejoy is manning the ice cream booth. Lisa Simpson, by far the most gifted and probing of the Simpson clan, approaches the stand, only to notice that the different flavors of ice cream are not identified in the usual fashion but have been given the names of different religious denominations. In her usual thoughtful manner she pauses, and then says, "I'll try the 'Unitarian.'" Lovejoy hands Lisa a bowl. She looks at it and says, "But there's nothing in here." Lovejoy's response: "That's the point." Instead of "productive emptiness," one might call this just "empty emptiness."

As far as I can tell, Unitarian jokes represent a growth industry, but this one happens to be particularly useful for our purposes. Let's make a third approach to the notion of the empty bowl, a notion that we can well symbolize with the central focus of the Unitarian Universalist sanctuary, the chalice. There is indeed a sense in which the chalice is empty: it is empty in the sense that it does not come pre-filled with congealed ideologies and elaborate doctrinal prohibitions. But *this* emptiness is, paradoxically, a precondition for fullness. One is free to become a part of the Unitarian Universalist community and to bring with herself or himself any number of different spiritual foci. In the next chapter, we shall concentrate on five, namely, humanism, nature, the arts, social justice, and the idea of a Creative Source/ Abyss of the universe. Every one of these, and many more besides, can be poured into the Unitarian Universalist chalice and can help to keep its flame alive.[4]

The issue before us, then, is just how it is possible to undertake our solitary journeys *together*. What is it that allows so many diverse spiritual disciplines to happily coincide within one chalice? Can we find some identity-in-difference in Unitarian Universalism, so that truly different spiritual ways may exist side by side in a community that confers upon each social plausibility and, thus, the aura of reality? I believe that there is indeed such an underlying unity, and that we can find it in a model of the spiritual quest that is built upon *participation* and *self-transcendence*. The spiritual quest is a quest to become something more than we already are, to participate in a reality larger than ourselves. Participation and self-transcendence are part of what it means to be human, and they go on everyday in a mundane fashion. While I am surely a unique individual, my being is also affected, for example, by the fact that I live in American suburbia. But participation in suburban mores is hardly the sort of participation, and hardly leads to the kind of self-transcendence, that most seekers have in mind. Instead, the spiritual quester's goal often goes so far as to fit Frederick Streng's definition of religion: "a means to ultimate transformation."[5] I might participate in reason and the human project; in nature; in the arts; in the struggle for social justice; or in the creative Source/Abyss of the universe. If my participation is part of a self-conscious and disciplined spiritual quest, then it will be an avenue to self-transcendence. This self-transcendence by no means needs to be masochistic or self-diminishing. Rather, it is a matter of "losing the [lesser, egotistical] self in order to find the [true] self," as Jesus puts it in the Gospels (Matthew 10:39). It involves looking beyond the merely phenomenal self and finding the Atman, the deep self that is identical with Brahman, the Godhead, as the *Upanishads* would have it.

This general structure of participation and self-transcendence is both substantive and nearly universal: it will be the particular combination of diverse ways of participation and self-transcendence that will make the U.U. path unique. But first we must figure out just why this general structure is in fact universal. We can find both negative and positive reasons for why people seek participation and self-transcendence. In his justly famous book *The Future of an Illusion*, Sigmund Freud offered three major reasons why people want to believe in God (belief in God being the form of participation and self-transcendence most familiar to a Viennese thinker of the early twentieth century). People desire to believe in God, said Freud, because they want to be protected from the terrors of nature; they want to be reconciled to the cruelties of fate, especially death; and they want to be rewarded in the hereafter for putting up with society's rules and prohibitions. Of course, Freud was convinced that there was no good evidence for God's existence, hence the wish to believe in God was just that, merely a wish. Inasmuch as Freud defined a belief based solely on a wish as an illusion, religion ends up as one big illusion, one psychologically childish desire for a supernatural father figure.[6]

Freud's negative verdict on religion and spirituality does not necessarily disqualify his diagnosis of the motives for the spiritual quest. We are finite, and finitude brings with it a host of ills. We naturally look for a way to transcend those ills. The twentieth-century Christian theologian Paul Tillich, despite his religious convictions, advanced a theory similar to Freud's, though Tillich's treatment is undeniably more subtle.[7] Why do we seek participation and transcendence? Because we are hemmed in by the circumstances of our fate. Because we know that we must die. Because we fall short of what we take to be our ethical responsibilities. Because our lives are never quite as full of meaning as we would like. Each of these problems, these threats to our being, says Tillich (following the lead of other philosophers before him), is given to the mind via that strange mood that we call "anxiety." Or, to make it sound deeper and even more ominous, we could employ the German version, *"Angst"*! This is not "pathological" anxiety says Tillich (under which heading we find anxiety about spiders, about bridges, about flying, and the like), but "existential" anxiety, that is, an anxiety about threats built into the very nature of human existence. This is the anxiety of W.H. Auden's *Age of Anxiety* or of Edvard Munch's *The Scream*.

If we cast our net more widely in time and space, we discover that the Buddha, for example, can chime in on the same initially pessimistic note as Freud and Tillich. After all, what were the Four Passing Sights, the specific things that set Sidharttha Gotama off on his quest for enlightenment? They were a decrepit old man, a diseased man, a corpse, and a monk who had withdrawn from the world and sought a better way. And what of the Preacher from the Book of Ecclesiastes in the Hebrew Bible/Old Testament? He famously tells us, in essence, "Eat, drink, and be merry, for tomorrow you die."[8] If the phenomena put before us in such unvarnished fashion by Freud, Tillich, the Buddha, and the Preacher of Ecclesiastes do indeed represent what finite flesh is heir to, then why not seek something more, something beyond? Why not seek self-transcendence, ultimate transformation, nirvana?

But that is the negative portion of the story. There is a positive dimension as well. The human spirit is open-ended. That means not that it has unlimited powers of knowing, but that it can always imagine something more or something higher. After all, we have come up with the idea of the infinite, the absolutely unlimited.[9] The world's religions tend to agree that our deeper nature is aimed at the infinite and that we shall not be content until we find it. More modestly, as Unitarian Universalists, we might aver that we are aimed at the infinite and that we shall not be satisfied unless we continually *pursue* it.[10] The human spirit, when healthy and energetic, naturally desires to live not in a claustrophobic, constricted thought-world, but in a "world with windows" in the evocative phrase of sociologist of religion Peter Berger.[11]

This open-endedness of the human spirit and its concomitant pursuit of something more ought not to be confused with a naively optimistic picture of the human *moral* condition. As has often been observed, recent human history has provided the unhappiest of insights into that of which human beings are capable: the Armenian Genocide, the Nazi Holocaust, Stalin's gulags, the reign of terror by Pol Pot, the internment of Japanese Americans during World War II, fascism and apartheid in South Africa, the prison scandals in Iraq. The list seems to go on and on, literally *ad nauseam*. But despite the moral squalor that we produce for ourselves, our spiritual quests might, we hope, still be able to rise, like the lotus flower, relatively unblemished out of the muck in which they are rooted.

The well-nigh universal status of the structure of participation and self-transcendence is reinforced by considering the world religions, which, we recall, are among the "Sources" for our Unitarian Universalist spiritualities. In a major strand of Indian religion, one seeks to throw off the finite world of illusion, of *maya*, and to participate in Brahman, the Godhead. In this case one attains a potent form of self-transcendence indeed, for as the *Upanishads* say, "Thou art That," in other words, you are the Godhead. The Buddhist seeks a radical form of self-transcendence by recognizing the finite self as an illusion and extinguishing that illusion so that he or she may participate in that mysterious infinite state known as nirvana. The Taoist, as we have seen, transcends the finite ego and has its place taken by the infinite power of the Tao, in which she now participates. The "religions of the book," namely, Judaism, Christianity, and Islam, all seek to overcome the self-centeredness that Martin Luther so picturesquely called "incurvedness" and to participate in God or Allah, to be "born again" in a new form of selfhood that completely transcends the ego with which one began.

We also find a clue to the perhaps inevitable ubiquity of the model of participation and self-transcendence in a rather unlikely source: contemporary brain research. Andrew Newberg and his associates have received a good deal of attention, even in the popular media, for their ventures into so-called "neurotheology." Newberg's research has concentrated upon brain scans of meditation adepts, from Buddhist monks to Catholic nuns. Previous studies of meditation have shown such modest effects as lowered respiration and blood pressure. But Newberg's claim is that in deep meditation, brain scans show a significant quieting of the posterior superior parietal lobe, what he has dubbed the brain's "orientation association area." The heart of his thesis is that, in deep meditation or religious experience, the boundaries of the self (the sense of which are controlled by the orientation association area) are expanded to the point that one experiences total oneness with a reality far beyond the self.[12] In short, we seem to have a biological, neurological basis for the phenomenon of participation and self-transcendence.

We are now in a position to return to the uniquely Unitarian Universalist symbol of the chalice. A chalice is the sort of cup that has a large-diameter rim and a capacious basin, its very shape advertising its inclusiveness: the Unitarian Universalist chalice can hold innumerable versions of the spiritual quest for participation and self-transcendence, and each makes its contribution to the life of the flame. Our chalice, then, holds a happy pluralism, a unity-in-difference made possible by the common structure of participation and self-transcendence found underneath diverse spiritualities. But we have not yet gone far enough in our philosophical interpretation of Unitarian Universalism. For it turns out that *this pluralism itself offers, on a second level, a further opportunity for participation and self-transcendence.* Here we begin to grasp something of the uniqueness of the Unitarian Universalist experience. For while there is indeed a general, underlying structural unity among spiritual quests provided by the elements of participation and self-transcendence, Unitarian Universalism is unusual in taking advantage of this structural unity by putting together diverse quests within a single community and affirming each. This experiment requires the mindset that has, from the beginning, conferred upon Unitarianism and Universalism the label "liberal religion." And this putting-together leads to a new, second level of participation and self-transcendence. The experience of being confronted with beliefs vastly different from one's own within one's own religious community, while it might lead some persons only to self-doubt, can instead be an exercise in expansion of religious consciousness. Others' beliefs and practices challenge my own in a way that enriches my understanding, not only "correcting" but also offering new material for my spiritual quest. And this openness to what others have to offer, even to the point, perhaps, of modifying or abandoning some of my own previous perceptions, is certainly a concrete instance of genuine self-transcendence. Pluralism itself becomes a motor of participation and self-transcendence.[13]

This effect of confronting the many different paths trod by my fellow questers is built upon a productive tension between the can and the cannot: I *cannot* attain a grasp of *everything* that any of those other paths has to offer, nor even a *superficial grasp* of all of them. On the other hand, I *can* attain a small grasp of at least some of what my fellow seekers are up to, thus being challenged to stretch my own spiritual sensibilities, challenged to self-transcendence. In this scenario, in this tension between the can and the cannot, we are putting our emphasis on the *can*, on the fact that we can attain further self-transcendence here. At the end of Chapter Two, we shall return to this tension, but there we shall emphasize the *cannot* side of the polarity.

Consider the following metaphor for this process of encountering the many different paths within my U.U. community. Suppose that you have an ordinary piece of paper before you on your desk. You draw a polygon on the paper, that is, a many-sided figure. Let us say that it is an octagon; it looks like a stop sign. But now suppose that you go to the extraordinary time and effort to draw a polygon with one hundred sides on your modest piece of paper. This new polygon will be almost indistinguishable from a circle. For here is a mathematical truth about polygons: the more sides are added, the closer a polygon will approach a circle, yet without ever becoming a circle, no matter how many sides are added. The circle, of course, is a symbol of completion, and even of infinity; it has neither beginning nor end. Here is how this mathematical phenomenon works as a metaphor: the more spiritual perspectives we encounter and in which we can participate, the closer we approach genuine spiritual wholeness, without ever perfectly reaching that state. Many-sidedness—in other words pluralism—points us in the general direction of the consummation of the spiritual quest, consummation as an ever-unattainable but eminently worthy goal. Unitarian Universalism is the hundred-sided polygon. And so we return yet again to our chosen symbol, to the chalice: the circular rim of the chalice suggests how our encounter with religious pluralism in Unitarian Universalism beckons us toward completeness, toward a productive expansion of spiritual consciousness, a most potent form of participation and self-transcendence. Thus, the *unity*-in-difference that is all-important in Unitarian Universalism's ability to midwife the rebirth of the sacred is only strengthened by the fashion in which U.U. pluralism calls each of us beyond our own idiosyncratic pieties. The identity of identity-in-difference is not simply the function of an underlying formal unity among spiritual paths provided by the structure of participation and self-transcendence. This identity is reinforced by the challenge by my co-questers to connect my spiritual quest, even in its content, with theirs.

Notes for Chapter One

[1] Huston Smith, *The World's Religions* (New York: HarperCollins, 1991), p. 207.

[2] *Chuang Tzu: Basic Writings*, trans. Burtson Watson (New York:

Columbia University, 1964), p. 113.

3   Of course, we need to be careful about what a Taoist might mean
by "right actions," since the Taoist will avoid any sort of strict
dualism of good and evil, a fact evidenced in the famous philosophy
of yin and yang. Things that appear to be opposites and that we
ordinarily strive to keep apart, from hot and cold to female and
male, are ultimately complementary and all necessary to the harmony
of the universe.

Despite its differences from Western theism, Chuang-Tzu's
advice does have a rough parallel in traditional Christianity. The
Christian ethic has sometimes been summed up by saying, "Love
God, and do as you please." This does not mean that loving God is
all that matters and that, with this duty fulfilled, one may go on to
wreak havoc. Rather, it suggests that one who loves God will,
precisely due to the infusion of that love in his life, automatically
want to do the right thing in each circumstance.

4   Discussion of Calvinist theology should, if possible, be avoided in
polite U.U. company. Now Calvin's place on the "Do-not-invite"
list is certainly understandable. First of all, the rigidities of Calvinist
orthodoxy constituted the major opponent battled by our universalist
and unitarian foremothers and forefathers in Colonial America.
But consider also Calvin himself. He taught the doctrine of Double
Predestination, according to which God had determined from all
eternity that certain human beings would be condemned to an eternal
Hell, a position that anyone with universalist sympathies found
anathema. And Calvin saw to it that the unitarian Michael Servetus
was put to death, an act hardly calculated to endear him to the
unitarian community.

But it is a delicious irony that John Calvin too made use of the
image of the empty bowl! Faith, said Calvin, is an "empty vessel."
Here is what he meant: the theological battle cry of the Reformation
was "Grace alone!" That is, one is saved simply by God's grace, not
by any good works that one can achieve. Even faith in this gracious
God is not a good work that the believer performs. Rather, it is a
wholly passive stance, an empty vessel that receives what God
reveals. This doctrine that salvation is only through grace, never

through human action, might have led to a Christian version of *wu-wei* or to universalism, but in Calvin's case it led to Double Predestination (with a little help from the fourth- and fifth-century Church Father Augustine of Hippo). Note too that Calvin's empty vessel is only empty of *human* works: it is immediately filled with all of the alleged contents of divine revelation.

It will be a cold day in that Hell to which Double Predestination condemns so many of us, then, before we can turn John Calvin into a Taoist. Indeed, *even Winnie the Pooh has been made an honorary Taoist before Calvin!* Need one say more? (I am referring, of course, to Benjamin Hoff's book, *The Tao of Pooh* [New York: E.P. Dutton, 1982].)

5   See Frederick J. Streng, *Understanding Religious Life*, third ed. (Belmont CA: Wadsworth, 1985), p. 2.

6   See Sigmund Freud, *The Future of an Illusion*, trans. James Strachey (New York: Norton, 1961). We face a strange divide in assessing Freud's importance in Western culture. On the one hand, his thought continues to spark creative discourse in literature, art, philosophy, and religion. But, ironically enough, in his chosen field of psychiatry Freud is undeniably a has-been. The field has largely moved away from Freud's psychoanalysis to a much more medically and scientifically oriented approach to the mind. Freud may have been convinced that he was a scientist, but how does one scientifically falsify or verify something such as the Freudian interpretation of dreams? For a hard-nosed critique of the Freudian legacy, see Frederick Crews, ed., *Unauthorized Freud: Doubters Confront a Legend* (New York: Viking, 1998). There are some, however, who maintain that even Freud's legacy as a scientist may be rehabilitated and made to cohere with contemporary neuroscience. For this contention, see Mark Solms, "Freud Returns," in *Scientific American* (May 2004): 82-88.

7   See Paul Tillich, *The Courage to Be* (New Haven: Yale University Press, 1952). Paul Tillich will pop up from time to time throughout this study. Why Tillich? There are at least three characteristics of Tillich's thought that make it an important resource for U.U. intellectual exploration. First, Tillich is one of the most philosophical

of contemporary theologians. Thus, he can provide a host of resources for our theorizing. Second, Tillich's thought is unusually ecclectic, drawing on everything from ancient Stoicism, to Reformation Christianity, to Japanese Buddhism. What could be better for studying the spiritual pluralism at issue in this book? Finally, Tillich is something of a fellow-traveler with U.U.s in that he is a decidedly liberal or even radical theologian. He is reported to have told the radical "death of God" theologian Thomas J.J. Altizer always to remember that "the real Tillich is the radical Tillich." His thought powerfully informs the work of radical feminist theologians such as Mary Daly and Carol Christ. It is no accident that the scholar often tapped as the most important Unitarian thinker of the twentieth century, James Luther Adams, learned from Tillich, wrote about him, and even presented Tillich's early German scholarship to the American public. See James Luther Adams, *Paul Tillich's Philosophy of Culture, Science, and Religion* (New York: Harper and Row, 1965).

[8]   See Ecclesiastes 8:15.

[9]   The seventeenth-century philosopher René Descartes, usually regarded as the father of modern Western philosophy, actually took this fact as a proof of God's existence. Our finite minds could never concoct the idea of the infinite. Thus, the fact that we do have that idea can only be explained by supposing that the notion of the infinite has been given to us by an infinite being, namely, God.

[10]   In the eighteenth century, Gotthold Ephraim Lessing said that if God held in one hand the entire Truth and in the other the eternal pursuit of Truth, Lessing would choose the latter. Perhaps we should make him an honorary Unitarian Universalist.

[11]   See Peter Berger, "For a World with Windows," in *Against the World for the World: The Hartford Appeal and the Future of American Religion*, edited by Peter L Berger and Richard John Neuhaus (New York: Seabury, 1976), pp. 8-19.

[12]   See Andrew Newberg, Eugene D'Aquili, and Vince Rause, *Why God Won't Go Away: Brain Science and the Biology of Belief* (New York: Ballantine, 2002).

[13]   John A. Buehrens, past President of the Unitarian Universalist

Association (1993-2001), makes essentially the same point in his Preface to *The Unitarian Universalist Pocket Guide*, 3rd edition, ed. John A. Buehrens (Boston: Skinner House, 1999), p. x.

Chapter Two

Five (and More)-in-One

There are many possible avenues to participation and self-transcendence in the spiritual quest, but we must be satisfied to examine five that seem to be particularly well-trod pathways today specifically within Unitarian Universalist communities:

(1) humanism,

(2) nature,

(3) the quest for social justice,

(4) the arts, and

(5) a Creative Source/Abyss of the Universe.

It must be made abundantly clear here at the outset that these five foci are not mutually exclusive. We are separating them artificially, simply for the sake of clarity. In actual practice, a Unitarian Universalist may attach importance to any combination of the five foci, and to other foci as well. The liberal religious community will, in any case, suggest that, whatever one's own chosen pathway, one should support one's sisters and brothers as they traverse different ways. This support is part of what lends each path the aura of reality conferred by a social plausibility structure. That they can all be affirmed by the self-same community depends, at the most basic level, on that formal identity conferred by the structure of participation and self-transcendence studied in the previous chapter. Hence, we will need to find that structure in each of the five ways under discussion here.

We begin with humanism. By "humanism" we usually mean, in the most general of terms, that human beings are the measure of all things (an assertion made already in Ancient Greece by Pythagoras). There is no God to guide us, to provide us with our moral standards, or to protect us from harm. Early twentieth-century humanism, the brand that made the biggest impact on Unitarian Universalism, shared some of Freud's attitudes in *The Future of an Illusion*. We ought, said these humanists, to face the reality that we live in a world without God and abandon any childish wishes that a supernatural being will deliver us from all of our problems. Thus, the most famous early statement of humanist principles, "The Humanist Manifesto" of 1933, signed by Unitarians and others, explained that humanism would "discourage sentimental and unreal hopes and *wishful thinking*."[1] Recall that a belief based on wishful thinking is precisely what Freud meant by an "illusion."

It is hard to imagine Unitarian Universalism without humanism, for while non-humanist Unitarian Universalists may wish to hold onto elements of the supernatural, humanism's unwavering commitment to the untrammeled search for truth and the acceptance of only those propositions that can be backed up by reasonable argument is an essential part of Unitarian Universalism's investment in a mature and rational spirituality. Our U.U. Sources point us to "humanist teachings which counsel us to heed the guidance of reason and the results of science, and warn us against idolatries of the mind and spirit."[2] Yet, humanism had its critics within Unitarian circles from the beginning. Historian David Robinson's account is particularly helpful here. The humanistic attitude in Unitarianism, even before "humanism" was identified as such, is well summed up, as Robinson suggests, by nineteenth-century Unitarian James Freeman Clarke's naively optimistic portrait of "the progress of mankind onward and upward forever."[3] While such a worldview seemed unrealistic to many from the beginning, the humanist tendency to embrace an exuberant optimism about human capabilities and the human future was, for a great many persons, shattered by the utter barbarity of the First World War. Later twentieth-century events would do nothing to improve the situation. Robinson shows how perhaps the most important Unitarian thinker of the twentieth century, James Luther Adams, attempted to come to the rescue of Unitarian humanism by reshaping its emphasis. Humanism could not work, suggested Adams, without a potent element of commitment to *making* the world a better place. In other words, rather than naively assuming that it was somehow simply in the cards for the human community to proceed, in Clarke's formula, "onward and upward forever," the humanist must embrace serious moral commitments that would lead to making the world a more just place. Rather than the tragedies of the twentieth century leading to pessimism, they could and should, argued Adams, spur such serious moral commitment.[4]

If humanist optimism took a beating from World War I and on through World War II, humanism has found itself under attack for other reasons from the later twentieth century up to the present. Humanism has fallen on hard times in contemporary philosophical circles in particular, and here we see an important connection between issues essential to Unitarian Universalism and the intellectual currents that flow through the larger world outside uniquely U.U. concerns. Martin Heidegger is almost unanimously accorded the honor of being called the most influential philosopher of the twentieth century, and Heidegger, especially in his later thought, had little time for humanism. For Heidegger, humanism is an imposition of the human will upon the world that, cognitively speaking, chops the world up into discrete *beings* and misses the much more fundamental reality of *Being*, that which lets beings be.[5] When the philosophical center of gravity shifted in the later twentieth century from Heidegger's Germany to France, the attack upon humanism continued unabated. For influential French thinkers such as Michel Foucault, Jacques Derrida, and Jean François Lyotard, the problem with humanism is not so much that it blinds us to Being, but rather that it provides a wholly mistaken notion of what it means to be a human being. Garden-variety humanism asserts, indeed campaigns upon the notion, that the human person is master of his or her own destiny (I shall argue that *Unitarian Universalist* humanism displays an important difference from the garden-variety). But so-called "postmodern" thinkers, such as the Frenchmen mentioned above, tend to suggest that the self is much more a passive and shifting construction than the confident master of its own fate. Our old friend Freud lurks in the background here too. For rather than picturing the self as a wholly autonomous entity harmoniously centered around reason, Freud paints the self as a fragile construction constantly pushed off-center by unconscious forces not under the self's control. Psychoanalysis, Freud bragged, has, along with Galileo and Darwin, inflicted upon human megalomania one of its greatest blows: it has shown human beings that they are not master even in their own homes; the psyche is not under my control, but is pushed about by forces and events of which I may be totally unaware.[6] The postmodernists have picked up on this suggestion. For example, Derrida and his many intellectual acolytes hold that, rather than language being a tool at the human subject's disposal through which she can confidently communicate her autonomously generated thoughts, the subject is the *product* of language, the intersection of various linguistic forces in a particular culture. As a result, the human person cannot control even her own language, and therefore texts can always be "deconstructed" to show how their language escapes and even contradicts the intentions of their authors.

What is postmodernism exactly, then? Even from our brief account above, it should be evident that postmodern thought sets itself against the modern tendency (endemic to garden-variety humanism) to seek mastery, both a mastery over one's self and over the world. The modernists were confident that reason could unify the various components of the self, that the self could be "centered" around reason. And they believed that the scientific method and its technological spin-offs could master the external world. But, as we have seen, we are not in fact masters of our own souls, for the self is a fragile construction that is constantly pushed off-center by forces beyond the power of reason to control. The self is "de-centered." And, at least from the perspective of the most strident postmodern critiques, the notion of scientific mastery of the world has proven both dangerous and illusory. The idea of the postmodern can be extended into all dimensions of culture. For instance, postmodern architecture no longer seeks adherence to a single architectural dogma, a stylistic dictum intended to master architectural design. Rather, it is happy with buildings that display a pastiche of different styles, buildings that have a hint of the modern skyscraper here and a whiff of gothic rooflines there. Perhaps the earliest truly significant example of a postmodern building is Philip Johnson's famous "Chippendale-roofed" and pink-granite-clad skyscraper in Manhattan at 550 Madison Avenue (which is, as of this writing, the Sony building). Postmodern pastiche can be found in music too. Twentieth and twenty-first century experiments with polytonality and atonality are examples. And on the popular level, hip-hop and electro-jazz are often fueled by the technique of "sampling" and "remixing," throwing different ingredients from different times and places into the artistic stew.

If humanism is a product of the modern confidence in and desire for control, then humanism would seem to be in serious danger in a postmodern culture. But contemporary Unitarian Universalist humanism triumphs over postmodernist attacks, I would suggest, due to at least two factors: a fundamental weakness in the postmodern program, and a distinctive dimension of U.U. humanism. First, it may well be argued that the Achilles heal of postmodern critiques of humanism, and especially of the powers of human reason, comes in its frequent misconstruals of natural science. Science is of paramount importance to traditional humanism. It is humanism's central example of the progressive powers of the human mind. But the "postmodernist thinkers"—admittedly a generalization—tend to dismiss science as just one more story about the world, with no more objective grip on reality than any other sort of narrative. Postmodernism relativizes and, to some extent, de-legitimizes the scientific worldview. But philosophically savvy scientists who have taken the time to plow through some of the postmodernist literature make a convincing case that the postmodernists are simply not in a position to pronounce on science, for they frequently massively misunderstand the very meaning of contemporary scientific theories and formulae.[7]

Secondly, it should never be forgotten that U.U. humanism has always been a decidedly *religious* humanism. And this, I would argue, makes all the difference. Insofar as it is religious *humanism*, this perspective denies any supernatural reality. But inasmuch as it is a *religious* humanism, it is ever informed by wonder and hence also by a certain humility. This means that the picture of the human subject held by Unitarian Universalist religious humanists is not of a wholly autonomous and "centered" self. Rather, their human subject necessarily leads an interdependent existence. The scientific perspective unlocks the universe's secrets, but those secrets, once revealed, inspire a sense of awe at the vast cosmos and of our inextricable connection with and dependence upon that cosmos. Indeed, the result of the religious humanist program is precisely participation and self-transcendence. The humanist participates with other human beings in the ongoing search for truth. Think, for example, about how cooperative natural science is: only those theories are accepted the experimental evidence for which is reproduced in trial after trial by scientists around the world. And again, the world uncovered by science is one in which the humanist understands herself as participating in a thoroughly intimate fashion, a theme that will be reinforced when we look at the second focus below, nature.

This sense of participation, an awareness of being only one member of a much larger community of inquirers to which one is beholden, and of a well-nigh-infinite universe, necessarily leads to self-transcendence. Indeed, if properly directed, this self-transcendence can involve precisely that sort of moral commitment and self-transcendence that James Luther Adams called for. Thus it is that we can pour the fuel of religious humanism into the

Unitarian Universalist chalice, confident in the knowledge that it will sustain the participation and self-transcendence that we seek in all of the chalice's contents.

It is but a small step from humanism as a focus for the spiritual quest to nature as a spiritual focal point (though there are definitely those who would imbue nature with "vital" or even occult forces that humanism and science eschew). For, as we have just seen, the scientific attitude toward nature championed by many religious humanists unlocks the truth of our deep participation in the natural world. The Darwinian theory of evolution did us a huge service in this regard, of course, by showing us how we as human beings are inextricably connected with the entire kingdom of living things upon the earth. And in the twentieth century, physics and cosmology reinforced that sense of participation, tying our own personal histories to the history of the universe itself, all the way back to the Big Bang some 14 billion years ago. Nothing is more evocative of our sense of participation in the larger universe than the oft-cited fact that the carbon in our bodies, the element that is the cornerstone of all life on earth, was produced by fusion reactions within stars, which later exploded and seeded space with the building blocks of our own being. Indeed, science has brought us to the point where we can recognize the artificiality of talking about human beings over against the world of nature: we *are* nature.

All of these examples of participation in nature lead directly to opportunities for self-transcendence. I can no longer honestly see my own ego as the center of things. Rather, I occupy but one point in a whole web of living beings, and the atoms and molecules that constitute me are just an infinitesimal portion of the matter and energy that make up our universe.

Science can definitely be a launching pad for a sense of participation in nature, then, and for a resultant self-transcendence. But, strictly speaking, the sort of reverence toward nature found in many Unitarian Universalist circles goes beyond what science offers by itself. For instance, the scientific attitude, taken just in and of itself, is one of purely rational analysis. But the full spiritual attunement to nature that is sought means that we must move beyond the *rational-analytic mindset* characteristic of scientific experimentation to what the Buddhists call *mindfulness.*

Now we must always keep in view the fact that there is no contradiction between the rational-analytic mindset of science and a Buddhist mindfulness toward nature. They are clearly different from one another, but the former can provide sustenance for the latter. Mindfulness means focusing one's attention just on what is happening right now, or on what one is doing in the moment. Thus, the Vietnamese Buddhist teacher Thich Nhat Hanh has suggested the mindful practice of "Washing the Dishes to Wash the Dishes." As one set of commentators clearly explains it, "That is, one trains oneself to keep one's consciousness alive to the present reality, to focus attention on the here and now, on the miracle of the soap and the water and the dishes and the process, rather than rushing through the chore mindlessly to get to whatever is next."[8] The element of participation is undeniably present here: mindfulness means participating by being fully present. But self-transcendence too is an essential part of the mix. She who practices mindfulness seeks not only a "personal appropriation of reality" (as opposed to mere objective knowledge of it, an analytic-rationalistic knowledge), but also "self-transformation through a personal grasp."[9]

What we are concerned with here, though, is mindfulness specifically of nature and the resultant sense of participation in nature and self-transcendence. Once again, while science is the paradigm of analytic-rationalistic thought, it can provide an invaluable springboard for moving onto a mindful participation in nature. This fact has been powerfully demonstrated by cell biologist Ursula Goodenough and moral philosopher Paul Woodruff. In their provocative essay "Mindful Virtue, Mindful Reverence," they point out that, confining ourselves to biology alone, science can call us to be:

* mindful of our place in the scheme of things
* mindful that life evolved, that humans are primates

* mindful of the dynamics of molecular life and its emergent properties
* mindful of the fragility of life and its ecosystems
* mindful that life and the planet are wildly improbable
* mindful that all of life is interconnected
* mindful of the uniqueness of each creature
* mindful of future generations

Thus, for example, thanks to science "mindfulness of the body is no longer just about breathing and walking as in the original Buddhist practice; we are now able to contemplate as well the molecular and genetic underpinnings of the body and its evolution from simpler forms."[10]

Of course, one can find the catalyst for a mindful approach to nature not just in science, but as ever, in something such as the observations of the poet. What could be more delightfully mindful, for example, than Jorie Graham's observations of a river in the following lines?

> Watching the river, each handful of it closing over the next,
> brown and swollen. Oaklimbs,
> gnawed at by waterfilm, lifted, relifted, lapped-at all day in
> this dance of non-discovery. All things are
> possible. Last year's leaves, coming unstuck from shore,
> rippling suddenly again with the illusion,
> and carried, twirling, shiny again and fat,
> towards the quick throes of another tentative
> conclusion, bobbing, circling in little suctions their stiff
> presence[11]

There are many possible avenues to a mindful, reverent relation to nature, and each of them will involve a sense of participation in nature and the experience of self-transcendence as one identifies the self not as an isolated, monadic ego, but as something that is what it is only as being-in-nature. Certainly this powerful perspective, too, can confidently be added to the Unitarian Universalist chalice.

The quest for social justice is the third focus of the quest for participation and self-transcendence that we shall explore. In many ways, this is the easiest of the five foci to grasp. First of all, the commitment to social justice is one of the hallmarks of Unitarian Universalism. In the present day, this commitment is evident in everything from the struggle for justice for gays and lesbians to the witness against an American imperialism and militarism run amuck. Historically, the concern for social justice is well symbolized by the life-work of the Unitarian Lydia Maria Child. Child was an anti-slavery activist who published an *Appeal in Favor of That Class of Americans Called Africans* in 1833 and who went on to become editor of the *National Anti-Slavery Standard*. At the same time, she championed what has been called a "pragmatic feminism."[12] And the history of U.U. social concern is symbolized too by Universalism's 1917 document, "A Declaration of Social Principles," which was authored by Clarence Russell Skinner. It called for "an Economic Order which shall give to every human being an equal share in the common gifts of God," and for "a Social Order in which there shall be equal rights for all, special privileges for none, [and] the help of the strong for the weak until the weak become strong."[13] And, of course, the U.U. concern for social justice becomes enshrined in the Principles, which express a commitment to the "inherent worth and dignity of every person," "justice, equity, and compassion in human relations," and the "goal of world community with peace, liberty, and justice for all."[14]

Second, the social justice focus is easy to grasp, in that its relation to participation and self-transcendence is relatively obvious. It involves participating in the lives and needs of others, both imaginatively and concretely. When the great Rabbi Hillel was challenged to define Judaism while standing on one foot, in other words, as succinctly as possible, he replied, "Do not do to others what you would not want them to do to you. All the rest [of the Torah] is commentary." In other words, one must empathetically participate in the lives of others, seeing them as akin to oneself. And this focus just as clearly entails self-transcendence: we must move beyond our present selves on behalf of the needs of others. As an individual, I should share my abundance and, what is sometimes more difficult, share my time with those in need. And as a nation, the United States should move beyond its present intransigence and sacrifice short-term, selfish economic gain: it should, to take but one example, act on behalf of the earth and its air and agree with other nations to abide by the provisions of international clean-air and clean-water treaties.

Participation in the struggle for social justice turns ought to have a special role to play in the life of participation and self-transcendence: we may presume that, in our focus on humanism or nature or any other spiritual focus, we are genuinely engaged in the act of self-transcendence, but we might in fact be fooling ourselves. Perhaps our quest is merely a selfish drive for our own fulfillment. The concrete sacrifices demanded by a concern for social justice serve as a test of whether our self-transcendence is real or illusory. We are reminded by Jewish theologian Abraham Joshua Heschel that

> religious thinking, believing, feeling are among the most deceptive activities of the human spirit. We often assume it is God we believe in, but in reality it may be a symbol of personal interests that we dwell upon. We may assume that we feel drawn to God, but in reality it may be a power within the world that is the object of our adoration. We may assume it is God we care for, but it may be our own ego we are concerned with. To examine our religious existence is, therefore, a task to be performed constantly.[15]

Engagement in the struggle for social justice can keep us honest in our quest for self-transcendence.

The Unitarian Universalist ability to hold diversity within a supportive community has relevance not just because it is key to re-enchanting the world, but also where social justice is concerned. A small coterie of persons dedicated to a particular aspect of the struggle for a just society may have a hard time making their voices heard. As a small, loosely organized group, they have no access to the levers of power because no connections with the institutional-structural components of our society. But the Unitarian Univeralist community is, among other things, an "institutional" religion, however much some U.U.s might be horrified by the thought. The advantage here, of course, is that institutional organization and interconnection with the larger social and political structure allows U.U. desires for social justice to be heard by the powers that be. And that means that individual groups within the Unitarian Universalist community that would otherwise have no chance to make themselves heard now do have that chance.

The quest for social justice too needs to take account of the latest philosophical debates in the larger intellectual culture, where arguments about the basis for action on behalf of social justice have been vigorous for the past several decades. First of all, as a general reminder, we always do well to heed Martin Luther King's admonition that the person dedicated to the good will ever require

> a tough mind, characterized by incisive thinking, realistic appraisal and decisive judgment. The tough mind is sharp and penetrating, breaking through the crust of legends and myths and sifting the true from the false. The tough-minded individual is astute and discerning. He has a strong, austere quality that makes for firmness of purpose and solidity of commitment.[16]

Such tough-mindedness about social justice today means once more taking account, fortunately or unfortunately, of so-called postmodern theory. Here is the issue: theorists such as Jean François Lyotard maintain that there is no overarching truth about the human condition. Each culture, perhaps even each individual, has its own story or narrative to tell. There is no one, overarching "metanarrative" or master narrative, such as the ones proposed by Christianity or Marxism, into which all other narratives must be fit. Each narrative is essentially a world unto itself, and each thus has its own internal criteria of good and bad, just and unjust. Now some champion this postmodern perspective as liberating: if there is no one narrative that can master all of our other narratives, than there is no coercive story outside my own to which I am beholden. I am free.

But perhaps, in thinking about the quest for social justice in particular, things are not quite so simple. Doesn't the project of liberation in fact require something at least akin to universal principles? Don't the Unitarian Universalist Principles depend on something universal? If we come upon another culture in which women are denied an education, prevented from entering the workforce, and generally seen as their husband's property, are we really just to walk away saying, "Well, that's what they do in their culture; what's wrong for us isn't necessarily wrong for them"? Similarly, if I come upon a self-enclosed, rampantly racist white subculture somewhere in the U.S., should I say, "While American culture as a whole has rejected racism, this community has created its own coherent social world, its own narrative, and within that narrative, lynching African-Americans is okay"? It looks as if true liberation is going to require some generally agreed upon principles, something that goes against the grain of the postmodernist phobia about metanarratives, such that it is possible to say that it is just wrong, in all times and places, to be bigoted against other human beings and brutally to kill them.

An important American philosopher and public intellectual who has combined an engagement with the latest trends in philosophical discourse with the quest for social, especially racial, justice is Cornel West. West's *The American Evasion of Philosophy*, for example, explores the peculiarly American philosophical school known as pragmatism, a school best represented, perhaps, by the paradigmatically liberal thinker John Dewey.[17]

Our fourth focus is the arts as an arena for participation and self-transcendence. It would be hard to identify something as a religion or as a spiritual practice if it were not accompanied by the devices of symbol, myth, and ritual. In the present day and age, symbolism and mythology and ritual are less often the product of unconscious social dynamics and more often a function of self-conscious artistic production. What is there about the arts that make them fertile ground for the spiritual quest, specifically for the phenomena of participation and self-transcendence?

The key is to be found, I think, in how we can be "taken up" into an artistic production.[18] We participate in an artwork and "inhabit" the world of the novel or of the film or play; we are "moved," even "carried away" by a piece of music; a painting or sculpture may afford us a "new way of seeing" the world. All of these expressions suggest the all-important dynamic of being carried beyond one's ordinary experience and perceptions, one form of self-transcendence. The most appropriate term of all here may well be "ecstasy," because of its religious connotations and its etymology. We know that the spiritual quest sometimes results in ecstasy: it is attested by everyone from Western mystics such as Teresa of Avila to Buddhists who attempt to describe nirvana. The word "ecstasy" comes from the Greek and means, literally, "to stand outside of," i.e., to stand outside of one's ordinary state of consciousness. It is akin, then, to "being beside myself."

Theologian Paul Tillich can once again provide us with some help here. In his discussion of genuine symbols, which can include works of art, Tillich tells us that art can open up dimensions of reality in correlation with dimensions of the human spirit.[19] Let us take a famous painting as an example, namely, Vincent VanGogh's *Starry Night*. The painting has been reproduced so many times and placed on so many mundane objects that it has probably lost some of its power to shock us, but suppose that we look again. We see the night sky, not as in a photo-realistic depiction, but as a frenetic juxtaposition of blazing, oversized stars, stars that look more like whole galaxies. A skeptic might wish to dismiss the painting as the hallucinatory vision of a deeply troubled painter, but surely it is much more than this. For what the painting uncovers, and that into which it takes me up, is that which stands behind and fructifies the night sky as it actually appears to the eye. That is, we see the raw power, the overwhelmingly intense energy behind the visible cosmos. As Tillich would say, the painting thus opens up a new dimension of reality, and the opening of reality must always be correlated with a moment of self-transcendence, with what Tillich calls the opening up of a new dimension of the human spirit. Leonardo and Picasso and VanGogh and O'Keefe and Nevelson can open up reality for those "who have eyes to see," a phrase Jesus uses to powerful effect in the New Testament to refer to spiritual attunement, to a particular kind of mindfulness. And to follow through on Jesus' language, we must not forget "those who have ears to hear": if there is any phenomenon that seems to be directly wired to our deepest emotions and perceptions of the world, it is music. It too can open up dimensions of reality in correlation with the human spirit, whether it comes from the mind of Handel, or Hindemith, or Jimi Hendrix.

Some have argued that abstract painting and sculpture, in particular, can open up the sacred. The historian of religions Mircea Eliade suggests that an abstract canvas (a Rothko, for example) is an exercise in breaking reality down into its fundamental building blocks, such as line, color, and movement. This is, says Eliade, to get down to the primal elements that give reality energy and life; it is to make contact with that which vivifies the world. Drawing upon his vast knowledge of religious rituals from around the globe, Eliade compares this process to the rites of spring carried out by many ancient peoples. The notion was that these rituals were essential: they had to be done so that the fructifying powers of the world could once again be unleashed and bring life back to the earth. Only in this way could the community, and the very earth itself, participate in the fundamental powers of being.[20] The arts are just as powerful for us today, just as often avenues to participation and self-transcendence. This is particularly true in Unitarian Universalist circles, I think. Precisely because Unitarian Universalists are bound by neither prescriptive dogmas nor constricting liturgical traditions, their gatherings can be informed by a plethora of different art forms. Whether it be dance, or jazz, or abstract sculpture in the sanctuary, Unitarian Universalist life is open to the enrichment made possible by even the most cutting-edge and experimental art forms. While former New York mayor Rudolf Giuliani may have taken deep offense at a painting of the Virgin Mary that was smeared with cow dung, I have not the slightest doubt that, while some within the U.U. community might respond as Giuliani did, others would be open to finding important religious commentary in that art work, as they would be open to finding a fierce beauty in the work of Robert Mapplethorpe.

Finally, what of the fifth focus for U.U. participation and self-transcendence? While many Unitarian Universalists, the humanists among them, may have no interest in a grounding for the universe beyond the basic forces of physics, many others look to a Creative Source/Abyss that transcends the merely physical. Historically speaking, of course, both universalism and unitarianism began with an uncompromising theism. Indeed, the defining teachings of both groups were *about God* (specifically, the Christian God). The unitarian position is that God is radically one—hence the name—and that therefore only God the Father is fully divine. The Son, Jesus Christ, is either a super-human creation of the Father or simply a man. The Christian Church did not officially define the doctrine that Christ was fully God until the Council of Nicea, called by the Emperor Constantine, in the year 325 of the Common Era. The full-blown doctrine of the Trinity, wherein the Holy Spirit would get in on the act, came along yet later. Many Christians of the early centuries of the Common Era, then, were, strictly speaking, unitarians. Closer in time to the unitarian movement that would come to birth in the United States was the anti-Trinitarian position articulated during the Protestant Reformation by Spaniard Michael Servetus, who was put to death in Geneva under the auspices of John Calvin.

Universalists maintained, over against traditional Christian teaching on Hell, that God would, at least eventually, bring all persons to salvation. While Colonial American universalism developed in response to the harsh Calvinist teaching about Hell and predestination that passed as orthodoxy in New England Congregationalism, hints of universalist thinking can be found much earlier.[21] The Church Father Origen, usually regarded as the most brilliant and most important of the early Greek Fathers, taught the "restoration of all things": through a process akin to reincarnation, God would in the end redeem all creatures, including even the Devil.

Despite the effects of secularization and disenchantment, there is still plenty of room today within the encompassing Unitarian Universalist chalice for belief in God, but that belief in God is itself bound to be pluralistic. And we shall encounter belief in dimensions of reality that, while they function as Source, cannot adequately be designated "God." In short, a glance inside our wide-mouthed chalice will reveal everything from belief in God to the quest for harmony with the Tao to a focus upon Buddhist Nothingness. Each of these versions of adherence to the notion of a Source/Abyss—it is where Buddhist nothingness, in particular, is concerned that it is best to refer to our focus as the Creative Abyss—is a powerful object of participation and self-transcendence.

Nothing more effectively summarizes the participation and self-transcendence at issue in belief in the Jewish, Christian, and Muslim God than the traditional Jewish confession known as the *Shema* (taken from the Book of Deuteronomy in the Hebrew Bible or Old Testament): "You shall love the Lord your God with all your heart, and all your soul, and all your might" (Deuteronomy 6:5). It was on the basis of this confession that our by-now-familiar theological adviser Paul Tillich came up with his influential definition of faith as "ultimate concern." One participates in the deity via this ultimate, unconditional commitment to Him or Her, and one is taken out of his ordinary mode of existence; one's life is rearranged; one experiences self-transcendence. The moment of self-transcendence is emphasized in the parables of Jesus found in the New Testament. Those parables, avers Jesus scholar John Dominic Crossan, always contain a moment of "reversal" wherein one's previous way of life and understanding is set upon its head.[22] Thus, for instance, the Samaritan—Palestinian Jews considered Samaritans second-class citizens at best—becomes "good."

The movement of theistic participation and self-transcendence come to their logical conclusion, many have argued, in what is called mysticism. Mysticism can be defined technically as the attempt to attain a direct relationship to God, so that one actually gets taken up into the being of God in Godself. One finds such mysticism, to mention only the most prominent examples, in one of the four traditional yogic paths of Hinduism (the four paths are laid out in the sacred Indian text known as the *Bhagavad Gita*, the "Song of God"); in the Jewish Kabbalah; among the Muslim Sufis; and within the history of Western, and especially Eastern, Christianity.

A Unitarian Universalist might also choose to engage in participation and self-transcendence via a less personal God. Here it is useful to return to the Tao, for the Tao is not a consciousness to which one might pray, but rather an infinite power that energizes the universe. As we saw in Chapter One, the goal of classic Taoist piety is to harmonize oneself with the Tao, so that the ego is shut down and one flows along with the very power of Reality itself. Some persons find this impersonal Source a more believable focus of devotion than a personal Supreme Being who consciously created the universe and who intervenes within the human world from time to time to alter the course of human history, or at least to give it a push in the right direction.

If I had a time machine, one of the persons whom I would certainly go back and visit would be Gotama Buddha. Despite its being an all-too-Western gesture, I would not be able to restrain myself from asking him if God exists. My guess, though, is that the Buddha would say, "It doesn't matter. Concentrate on the road to enlightenment." In one of his lesser-known films, *Stardust Memories*, Woody Allen's character encounters advanced extraterrestrials in the obligatory flying saucer, and he asks them, "Is there a God?" They reply that he is asking the wrong kind of question. While this scene is admittedly less lofty than an encounter with the Buddha—it ends accompanied by the strains of Glenn Miller's *Moonlight Serenade*—I am reasonably sure that the Buddha would agree with the aliens. Buddhism is not about God. Yet Pope John Paul II offended many in the contemporary Buddhist community when he wrote that Buddhism is a species of "atheism." How, then, do we sort out the Buddhist perspective on a Source, or a Creative Abyss, in which I might participate?

Allow me to attempt to answer this question, but with the caveat that I shall engage in well-nigh inexcusable generalizations. There is no *one* Buddhist philosophy; there are many Buddhist schools. We shall have to be satisfied, then, with something like the *Cliff Notes* guide to Nothingness in Buddhism (while reading only the *Cliff Notes* guide to *Moby Dick* when I have been assigned the novel itself will merely result in a low grade in literature class, lazily restricting oneself to the *Cliff Notes* on Buddhist thought undoubtedly results in frightfully bad karma).

Due in large part to the legacy of the Ancient Greek philosophers, Western thinkers are apt to see the world in terms of being, of substance and presence. Asian thinkers, by contrast, are much more willing to plumb the depths of nothingness. It is instructive in this regard to compare René Descartes, the seventeenth-century father of what is considered modern Western philosophy, and the Buddha. Descartes was philosophically obsessed with the question, "What can we know with certainty?" This passion for certainty probably sprang, in part, from the horror of the Wars of Religion that had ravaged Europe: differences of religious opinion—an evident lack of certain knowledge—had led to horrendous violence. Descarte's quest for certainty led him to his method of doubt: I shall, he said, doubt everything that I possibly can until I come upon something that is simply beyond doubt, something absolutely certain. And thus it is that Descartes settled upon his famous *Cogito ergo sum*, "I think, therefore I am." In other words, the one thing of which I am absolutely certain is my own existence, for in order to doubt, there has to be a doubter. The self is the most real thing, and on the basis of my certainty of it I can go on to establish knowledge of the external world and even of God.

The Buddha does not hold that the self is the most real thing. On the contrary, the Buddhist tradition tells us that the Buddha taught the doctrine of *anatman*, of "no self"! The finite self is ultimately an illusion, a mental construct that is created by putting together mere unrelated "heaps" of qualities, such as the body, the emotions, one's memories, and so on. The matter is akin to a sport such as football: what we call the "team" is not a tangible thing, not an independent substance that is out there in the world. Rather, the "team" is simply a mental construct put together out of the individual players that we see out on the field. No real team; no real self. Of course, the Buddha had a very practical reason for denying the reality of the self, and that is that the notion of the self is the source of all the attachments, all of the selfish cravings and desires, that lead to suffering. To extinguish the illusion of self, then, is to transcend suffering. One who has blown out the candle of selfhood will remain unperturbed in face of the Passing Sights witnessed by the Buddha, such as old age, disease, and even death.

But suppose that we push a bit further into Buddhist thinking. Perhaps nothingness resides not just at the heart of selfhood, but, in a sense, at the heart of all that "is." Here we inevitably encounter the Buddhist notion that all things are what they are just in their relation to other things. Thus, no thing has any independent character or substance. A football, to extend the example used above, is really a football only in the context of a particular game. In other contexts, it might be a weapon—think, for instance, about a good, tight spiral thrown directly and purposefully at your head—or it might serve as a toy for your Yellow Labrador to chew on.

We engage the realm of nothingness in earnest when we explore the philosophy of the Buddhist thinker Nagarjuna, who probably lived sometime between 150-250 C.E.[23] Nagarjuna emphasized the difference between conventional truth, which even he admitted we must use in our mundane dealings with the world, and Ultimate Truth. The Ultimate Truth is *sunyata*, that is, the "emptiness" of all things. There is no fundamentally real football, something that just is a football in and of itself. Rather, it is a football because we perceive it as such. The liberation that comes with the doctrine of *sunyata* is the familiar Buddhist freedom from attachment. But Nagarjuna takes this notion with particular seriousness. For him, even nirvana, the blissful goal of the Buddhist quest, is empty. If we were to reify nirvana as some sort of substantial state to be attained, then we would become attached to it in the same way that we become attached to other things, which is tantamount to saying that nirvana itself would become a source of turmoil!

Do I exemplify the model of participation and self-transcendence if I embrace the way of Buddhist emptiness as set forth by Nagarjuna? There can be little question about self-transcendence: I leave the very notion of ordinary selfhood behind as an illusion; the self is a mere mental construction. It is not as clear that there is any "thing" in which I can participate. Yet, if we really push Nagarjuna's line of reasoning, it would not be impossible to see emptiness as akin to the Tao, at least in practical, if not metaphysical terms. Emptiness here is productive, for it is like the empty space that makes a cup useful. That is why we have designated this emptiness or nothingness the Creative Abyss (recall *wu-wei*: "creative quietude"). Emptiness is the potential Source of my liberation from attachment and its attendant suffering.

It is even possible that the Western notion of Being and the Buddhist notion of emptiness start out in opposite directions at the bottom of a circle only to meet, in the end, at the top of that same circle. If Descartes was the most important Western philosopher of the seventeenth century (and Immanuel Kant of the eighteenth), the nod for that honor in the nineteenth century (a formative century for Unitarianism and Universalism in America) goes to the German thinker G.W.F. Hegel. At one point, Hegel opines that "Pure being and pure nothing are one and the same."[24] Nothingness, by definition, has no attributes via which

I can gain a conceptual hold upon it. But the same is true of
pure Being: having attributes is a characteristic of individual
beings, not of Being, which lets individual beings be. And it is
of more than passing interest that Christian theologians have
sometimes described God as pure Being. They can go clear
back to the Hebrew Bible/Old Testament story wherein Moses
asks God for God's name, and God replies "I AM" (Exodus 3:14),
an answer creatively interpreted by some philosophically inclined
Christian theologians to mean that God is Being. In the thirteenth
century, the paradigmatic Roman Catholic theologian Thomas
Aquinas identified God with *esse*, the pure act of being.

Might this mean that God, like emptiness or nothing, is
beyond description altogether? One traditional Christian
theological method known as the *via negativa*, the way of negation,
holds this to be so. We can only say what God is not, never what
God is. Even Saint Augustine (the progenitor of Calvin's Double
Predestination) proclaims that "If you understand him, it would
not be God."[25] These sensibilities are surely not far removed
from the dictum found at the beginning of the *Tao Te Ching* that
"The tao that can be told is not the eternal Tao."[26]

Of course, each of these ways of conceiving of a Creative
Source or Abyss of the universe draws upon quite traditional
religious sensibilities. We might attempt to stitch them together,
but the finished product will still bear the marks of age-old pieties.
And we have seen that these age-old pieties have been battered
by the forces of secularization. A good deal of their power has
been carried away by the ebb tides of the ever-receding traditional
Sea of Faith. The rebirth of the sacred may well manifest itself,
in the case of these pieties, then, by their being re-energized by
being held in productive tension with the other spiritual paths
affirmed within the Unitarian Universalist community.

We have considered five oft-employed foci for the spiritual
quest within Unitarian Universalism, and we have seen that each
exemplifies the structure of participation and self-transcendence.
This puts us in a position to look back at Chapter One. I would
argue that the common structure of participation and self-

transcendence does indeed suggest that the multiple contents that keep the chalice alight are not wholly disparate; they do not represent a chaotic juxtaposition of worldviews. Instead, they have a deep, underlying structure in common. We encounter identity-in-difference. Remember also that we argued in Chapter One that U.U. pluralism *itself* is a source for participation and self-transcendence. For by living in a community with a wide range of different spiritual quests and insights, my own limited perspective is potentially corrected and broadened. The common structure of participation and self-transcendence makes it *possible* to hold together within one religious community the five foci considered above. The liberal convictions of Unitarian Universalism lead U.U.s to *actualize* this possibility. As a result, plausibility and reality are bestowed on each of the five foci and more. The world is re-enchanted, and the sacred shows itself once more.

At the end of the previous chapter, we considered the power of self-transcendence provided by our encounter with the many spiritualities different from our own contained within the U.U. community. We saw that this dynamic was a function of a productive tension between the fact that we **can** grasp a bit of what is going on in those other spiritualities, even to the point of allowing them to affect our own, but that we **cannot** begin to plumb **all** that those other spiritualities have to offer. At the end of Chapter One we emphasized the *can* component of the dynamic. Now it is time to emphasize the *cannot*. For one of the ways in which Unitarian Universalist pluralism re-enchants the world is by confronting us with what I choose to call the Mysterious Depth of reality. That is, precisely by encountering all of the different spiritualities of my fellow seekers, I am overwhelmed by the *so-much-more of reality*, the so-much-more than I can ever understand. And precisely this can disclose the Mysterious Depth of what is.

Now this is not a mystery in the scientific sense. Scientific mysteries are simply things that we do not presently understand but may well understand in the future as our scientific knowledge advances. It is not a matter here, in other words, of some *physical* mystery about the cosmos. Rather, what I have in mind is a matter of *existential* mystery, the mystery of what human life is all about, how it should be lived and how fulfilled. The overwhelming diversity and richness of the spiritual ways that I encounter within the U.U. community convince me that I can never plumb the depths of these existential questions: I walk humbly, ever suspended above the Mysterious Depth.

It is worth noting, too, that this humble walk is something that all members of the community can share, despite the potentially great differences in their individual spiritualities. For each and every one of us can acknowledge the more that lies beyond our own spiritual perceptions, and thus each can encounter the Mysterious existential Depth of reality.

That we have not yet exhausted the symbolic power of the chalice is evident in the fact that, in addition to its other symbolic functions, it can represent the rebirth of the sacred and the disclosure of the Mysterious Depth. A chalice is a goblet, a cup with a stem. That stem, which runs between the chalice bowl and the base that, ultimately, connects it with the earth, is a species of what Mircea Eliade contends is a nearly universal fixture of human religiosity, the *axis mundi*.[27] The phrase "*axis mundi*" means literally the "axis of the world." In religious symbolism, it is a vertical structure—whether a pole or tree or mountain—that represents a pathway between the mundane and the sacred. The Jewish and Christian traditions are replete with examples of *axis mundi* symbolism. In the book of Genesis, we find the Tree of Life, the fruit of which can provide immortality. It suggests a way of transition between mere mortals and God. There is Jacob's ladder, which is pictured as a literal passageway between earth and the realm of the divine (a biblical version of our contemporary speculations about cosmic "wormholes," as it were).[28] The preeminent symbol in all of Christianity, the cross or crucifix, turns out to be another *axis mundi* symbol. It is the "tree"—a familiar expression in early Christianity—upon which Christ was put to death, and it was that death that atoned for sin and opened the gates of heaven.

Other religions too have their *axis mundi* symbolism. There is the pole at the center of some Native American tents; the Egyptian pyramids, which are meant as entryways to the next life, fit the bill as well; the ziggurat in ancient Babylon can also be taken as an *axis mundi* symbol. Our contemporary skyscrapers, as monuments to multi-national capitalism, are probably more akin to the Tower of Babel than to the *axis mundi*. But I take the classic rocket ship design to work for many of us, on the unconscious level, as a powerful *axis mundi*. Granted, the more cynical may read its symbolism in terms of the phallic violation of the heavens, but surely one can at least argue that there is something much more positive at work. The rocket ship symbolizes our desire to free ourselves from our gravitational tether and to become a part of the larger cosmos.

The stem of the Unitarian Universalist chalice, then, is one more *axis mundi* symbol, an access-way that leads from our ordinary way of being, with its spiritual inattention, to the reality of the sacred, to the Mysterious Depth. We gather in a vibrant, pluralistic community, the chalice standing before us, beckoning each of us to walk self-reliantly on a particular spiritual path. But, at the same time, we set off on our journey with the assurance that we are supported by the others gathered round about us, by other pilgrims on disparate paths. We are on a solitary journey together, a journey toward sacrality.

Notes for Chapter Two

[1]   "The Humanist Manifesto," in *The Epic of Unitarianism*, ed. David B. Parke (Boston: Skinner House, 1985), p. 141 (emphasis mine)

[2]   See *Singing the Living Tradition*, p. x.

[3]   Quoted in David Robinson, *The Unitarians and the Universalists* (Westport CT: Greenwood Press, 1985), p. 153.

[4]   See Robinson, *The Unitarians and the Universalists*, pp. 152-154.

[5]   Some might counter that Heidegger himself could have used a strong dose of humanism. His legacy is severely tainted by the fact that

he spent some time as a member of the Nazi party, that he spoke well of the Nazis, and that he never in later years clearly disavowed or apologized for his involvement. The major question for interpreters of Heidegger's thought is whether it leads one to Nazism, or whether it has no connection with Nazism and Heidegger's errors are simply the result of idiosyncratic immoral decisions with no connection to his philosophy.

6   See Sigmund Freud, *Introductory Lectures on Psychoanalysis*, trans. James Strachey (New York: Norton, 1966), p. 284.

7   The most important work here is probably Alan Sokal and Jean Bricmont, *Fashionable Nonsense: Postmodern Intellectuals' Abuse of Science* (New York: Picador, 1998).

8   Ursula Goodenough and Paul Woodruff, "Mindful Virtue, Mindful Reverence," in *Zygon: The Journal of Religion and Science* 36 (December 2001): 586.

9   Goodenough and Woodruff, "Mindful Virtue, Mindful Reverence": 587.

10   Goodenough and Woodruff, "Mindful Virtue, Mindful Reverence": 588.

11   Jorie Graham, "Notes on the Reality of the Self," in *The Dream of the Unified Field: Selected Poems 1974-1994* (Hopewell NJ: Ecco Press, 1995): 159.

12   See David Robinson, *The Unitarians and Universalists*, p. 128. On Unitarians' response to slavery, see also *A Stream of Light: A Short History of American Unitarianism*, 2nd edition, ed. Conrad Wright (Boston: Skinner House, 1989), pp. 40-43; 56-57.

13   See Charles A. Howe, *The Larger Faith: A Short History of American Universalism* (Boston: Skinner House, 1993), pp. 92-94.

14   *Singing the Living Tradition*, p. x.

15   Abraham Joshua Heschel, *God in Search of Man: A Philosophy of Judaism* (New York: Meridian, 1959), p. 9.

16   Martin Luther King, Jr., *Strength to Love* (Philadelphia: Fortress, 1981), p. 10.

17   *The American Evasion of Philosophy: A Genealogy of Pragmatism* (Madison: University of Wisconsin, 1989). See also Cornel West, *Race Matters* (New York: Random House, 1994).

18   The preeminent (and difficult) contemporary philosophical analysis of how one is taken up into a game or an artistic work is Hans-

Georg Gadamer, *Truth and Method*, trans. ed. Garrett Barden and John Cumming (New York: Continuum, 1975).

[19] See Paul Tillich, *Dynamics of Faith* (New York: Harper and Row, 1957), Chapter Three.

[20] Mircea Eliade, "The Sacred and the Modern Artist," in *Art, Creativity, and the Sacred*, ed. Diane Apostolos-Cappadona (New York: Crossroad, 1988), pp. 179-183.

[21] In a fitting irony, if not comeuppance, the thinker tapped as the greatest Calvinist theologian (many would say the greatest Protestant theologian, *period*) of the twentieth century, at least hinted at universalism. The Swiss theologian Karl Barth, who died in 1968, held to the Reformation line that salvation was only by grace. But rather than following this out to the conclusion that God must have therefore simply pre-ordained who was to be saved and who was to be damned, Barth pointed to a possible reworking of the Calvinist doctrine of Double Predestination: it was Christ who was predestined to punishment by God, to suffering on the cross. Humanity, in turn, thanks to Christ's atoning suffering, was predestined, one and all, to salvation.

[22] See John Dominic Crossan, *In Parables: The Challenge of the Historical Jesus* (New York: Harper and Row, 1973).

[23] A most helpful study of Nagarjuna is Frederick J. Streng, *Emptiness: A Study in Religious Meaning* (Nashville: Abingdon, 1967). The book's appendix contains translations of Nagarjuna's "Fundamentals of the Middle Way" and "Averting the Arguments."

[24] As it turns out, Hegel did not announce this truth in the spirit of happy discovery. On the contrary, it was meant as a put-down of some of his fellow philosophers, who depicted Being as finally ineffable. Hegel argued that, unless we can say something about Being (which he called the Absolute), if it is without any attributes, then it is indistinguishable from mere nothingness. We shall proceed undeterred, despite the critical intent of Hegel's utterance.

While the vantage point of history awards Hegel the honor of being the nineteenth century's most important philosopher, during the nineteenth century itself that honor belonged, at least according to many English-speaking philosophers, to Herbert Spencer. This is of interest simply because both Hegel and Spencer had important effects upon Unitarian thinkers. Hegel's claim that there was a faculty higher than mere "understanding," namely "Reason," via which one could directly intuit the Absolute or God, had a potent effect, at least indirectly, upon Ralph Waldo Emerson and the Transcendentalist movement that arose within Unitarianism. And Spencer's adaptation of Darwinian evolution to a wider evolutionary view of the universe informed the thinking of persons such as Francis Abbot, a leading Unitarian theologian of his day who published a book titled *Scientific Theism* in 1885. Abbott did not accept the whole of Spencer's evolutionary philosophy, however, for he thought it too mechanistic to cohere with his own theistic view. On Spencer and Abbott, see David Robinson, *The Unitarians and the Universalists*, pp. 113-116. And see Francis Ellingwood Abbot, *Scientific Theism* (London: Macmillan, 1886), available in reprint form from Elibron Classics.

[25] Quoted in *Catechism of the Catholic Church* (Rome: Urbi et Orbi, 1994), p. 61.

[26] *Tao Te Ching: A New English Version, with Foreword and Notes by Stephen Mitchell* (New York: Harper and Row, 1988), p. 1.

[27] See Mircea Eliade, *The Sacred and the Profane: The Nature of Religion*, trans. Willard R. Trask (New York: Harcourt, Brace, and World, 1959). Eliade's conviction that religions around the world, ancient and modern, share a common underlying structure of symbolism finds less favor among religious studies scholars today, who tend to emphasize the uniqueness and particularity of each tradition. Part of what fueled Eliade's convictions about commonality, and those of his more media-savvy contemporary Joseph Campbell, was the thought of Swiss psychoanalyst Carl Jung with his famous notion of the "collective unconscious" and its "archetypes."

[28] If not from the sublime to the ridiculous, then at least from the sublime to contemporary popular culture: the rock music classic *Stairway to Heaven* by Led Zeppelin clearly draws upon this ancient *axis mundi* symbolism. If one prefers a more recent and perhaps more artistically rarified example, one may turn to jazz-singer

Cassandra Wilson's "Seven Steps (to heaven)" on her Miles Davis tribute album, *Traveling Miles*. It is particularly interesting that Wilson chooses *seven* steps. Seven has often been taken to be a sacred number, and one sometimes hears the expression, "I was in seventh heaven!" presumably the highest level of heaven. According to the Muslim tradition, when Mohammed made his supernatural Night Journey to heaven from the Temple Mount in Jerusalem, he encountered seven heavens. Compare 2 Corinthians 12: 2-4 where, alas, poor St. Paul (or one of his acquaintances) is lifted up only to the third heaven.

Chapter Three

How the Sacred Re-Shows Itself

There the angel of the Lord appeared to him in a flame
of fire out of a bush . . . the bush was blazing yet it was
not consumed. Then Moses said, "I must turn aside and
look at this great sight" . . . . God called to him out of the
bush . . . . "Come no closer! Remove the sandals from
your feet, for the place on which you are standing is
holy ground."

—Exodus 3:2-5.

I say more: the just man justices;
Keeps grace: that keeps all his goings graces;
Acts in God's eye what in God's eye he is—
Christ. For Christ plays in ten thousand places,
Lovely in limbs, and lovely in eyes not his
To the Father through the features of men's faces.
—Gerard Manley Hopkins, "Inversnaid"[1]

When we turn from self and seek to be aware,
we will find holy light in human faces,
in blossom, birdsong, and sky.

—Alice Berry
Used in the U.U. Flower Communion[2]

In the early twentieth century, philosopher Edmund Husserl launched the movement known as phenomenology. The word "phenomenon" derives from the Greek word for that which appears or shows itself. The suffix of "phenomenology" is the Greek *logos*, which means word or reason. Thus, phenomenology is to be understood as reasoning about—the study of—how things show themselves to human consciousness. Husserl employed his phenomenology to uncover what he called "essences," though he had no particular interest in seeking after the essence of the sacred or how it shows itself to us. But religion scholars, such as Mircea Eliade, upon whose work we have already had several occasions to draw, immediately saw the promise of phenomenology for religious studies. Eliade realized that the sacred almost invariably shows itself, not directly, but through mundane objects, such as the bush of our biblical epigraph. The sacred appears "in, with, and under" the concrete realities of the everyday world, as Martin Luther described the presence of Christ within the elements of the Eucharist.

The Christian Eucharist, since it is a "sacrament," is a good jumping off point for our discussion in this chapter. For while Unitarian Universalists do not have sacraments per se, we shall see that there is much that is sacramental in their practice and experience. Traditional Christians have defined a sacrament as a visible sign of an invisible grace. Suppose we modify this for U.U. purposes to say that a sacrament is a visible sign of the (in itself) invisible sacred. Sacraments show the sacred within the concrete, the infinite within the finite. The Catholic sacraments, for example, utilize such concrete, physical elements as water, bread, wine, oil, the laying on of hands, and other physical gestures. Doesn't the sacred re-manifest itself in Unitarian Universalism, in the secular world, through equally concrete elements? Of the five foci studied in the previous chapter, for example, humanism, nature, social justice, and the arts surely involve concrete elements. And the underlying dynamic of U.U. re-enchantment is thoroughly sacramental, in that it is a result of my face-to-face interaction with other human beings who practice diverse spiritualities: "Christ,"—the sacred—appears, as Gerard Manley Hopkins would have it, in the faces of others.

These observations lead us to reflect on just what kind of "church"—I use the term in the generic sense of a faith community of whatever stripe—the Unitarian Universalist community is. A bit of historical perspective is in order here. The earliest Americans who held universalist or unitarian convictions were Protestant Christians. More specifically, the majority of them started out within New England Congregationalism, which was informed by Calvinist theology and practice. Now the first Calvinists were true iconoclasts: they took it as gospel that, as Calvin himself put it, the human mind is a constantly humming "factory of idols," in other words, that we are always in danger of falling into idolatry. "To God alone belongs the glory," shouted these zealous enemies of worshipping anything other than God. Hence, Calvinist theology emphasized God's transcendence to a much greater degree than his (and it was indeed "his" for these believers) immanence. And, of course, Calvinists would have nothing to do with popes or saints or veneration of the Virgin Mary. Regarding nature as in any way sacred would have been a pagan abomination in this setting, and it is not difficult to connect this particular sensibility with what can only be called a suspicion of the sacraments. While Roman Catholicism had, and still has, its seven sacraments, the Calvinists (basically following the lead of Martin Luther) cut the number down to two, specifically, baptism and the Lord's Supper. The ostensible reason for this reduction is that Protestantism is based on the authority of Scripture alone—the principle that the Reformers called *sola scriptura*—and that the only sacraments clearly initiated by Christ in the New Testament are baptism and Holy Communion. But there is something else at work here: sacraments emphasize not the transcendence of God, but God's immanence. In the sacraments, according to Christian theology, God shows Godself in physical, concrete media. We should not be surprised then to uncover a Calvinist suspicion of the whole sacramental principle. It is no accident that Calvin rejected the notion that the bread and wine of Holy Communion become the very body and blood of Jesus Christ, a notion affirmed by Roman Catholics and, with slight variation, by Lutherans. For Calvin, Christ is *spiritually* present in the Lord's Supper, but not literally, physically present. Furthermore, Christ is spiritually present *everywhere*.

The point of this story is that Unitarians and Universalists, as erstwhile Calvinists, have ended up on the opposite end of the church spectrum from where they began: Unitarian Universalism has become fully committed to the sacramental principle, the principle that the sacred shows itself in the most concrete of fashions, and most especially in the flesh and blood human beings with whom we cross paths in the spiritual quest. Though Unitarian Universalists by no means limit their Sources to Christ and Christianity, they ought to be able easily to understand feminist theologian Rosemary Radford Ruether's claim that

> In the language of early Christian prophetism, we can encounter Christ *in the form of our sister*. Christ, the liberated humanity is not confined to a static perfection of one person two thousand years ago. Rather, redemptive humanity goes ahead of us, calling us to yet incompleted dimensions of human liberation.[3]

For an early Unitarian gesture toward the idea that the mystery that is the sacred can be found within ourselves and our fellows, one need only look to Ralph Waldo Emerson's famous and controversial "Divinity School Address" of 1838.[4]

How does sacrality show itself within the Unitarian Universalist community? On one level, it does so through such concrete realities as our own reason, nature, the arts, and acts of social justice. But, as we have seen, the real key is the community itself, the gathering of liberal religious questers each of whom, while on her own individual journey, affirms the validity of the paths chosen by her neighbors, thereby contributing to the plausibility structure of their quests. Insofar as the sacred is made tangibly present in my interaction with fellow-travelers within my community, we can aver that the Unitarian Universalist community itself is sacrament. Though it may surprise some U.U. ex-Catholics, this assertion bears resemblance to the claim of Catholic theologians such as Karl Rahner and of the documents of the Second Vatican Council (1962-1965) that the Church is not simply a sacramental agent but is itself sacrament, the sacramental Body of Christ. At the same time, the Unitarian Universalist sensibility is not without a remaining Protestant and Jewish caution about too tightly linking sacrality and that through which it manifests itself. To hold these two sensibilities in tension, we must affirm a paradox: *that which cannot be seen shows itself.* We hold together an "is" and an "is not." The concrete U.U. community made up of flesh and blood human beings *is not* the sacred, but my fellow seekers are indeed the enabling mechanism, the source of the plausibility structure, through which the sacred *is* made manifest, whether in nature, in the arts, in acts of social justice, or somewhere else.

From the principle that the concrete community of U.U. seekers is itself a sacrament midwifing the rebirth of the sacred, we can move on to consider what particular acts or experiences within this community's gathering might qualify as a conduit of the sacred. The issue now is not the many different spiritual practices that individual seekers might choose to follow, each such practice manifesting the sacred so long as it receives the plausibility structure provided by the community, but rather rites and experiences that are part of the entire gathered community. We have already had ample opportunity to note how the chalice stands in for much of what Unitarian Universalism is all about. Of particular relevance here is the claim that the chalice stem is an *axis mundi.* As such, it manifests the sacred, the Mysterious Depth, or at least it is an access-way to the sacred.

What other examples of the sacramental principle are worthy of note? Unitarian Universalist eclecticism means that individual members or groups within the community may from time to time share particular rituals with the larger community. Some U.U. churches have services within which Wiccan ritual is a part; many celebrate the Jewish seder; most have Christmas celebrations. But we shall give attention to four especially significant examples of U.U. "sacramental" practice through which the sacred is reborn, namely, the Flower Communion, as well as the experiences of multi-dimensional sacred space, multi-faceted sacred time, and multi-vocative sacred language.

The Flower Communion

The Flower Communion was created by Czechoslovak Unitarian Dr. Norbert Capek, no doubt with help from his wife Maja Capek, in 1923. Both of the Capeks were Unitarian ministers. The Flower Communion becomes all the more poignant when we learn that Dr. Capek was martyred by the Nazis in Dachau for his humanitarian and egalitarian convictions. In the Flower Communion, practiced by many North American Unitarian Universalist congregations today, each member of the congregation brings a flower from his or her own garden or elsewhere and places it in a common vase. This bringing together of the contributions of all the members of the gathering symbolizes that their many individual ways and contributions add up to one community, one "communion." "Together the different flowers form a beautiful bouquet. Our common bouquet would not be the same without the unique addition of each individual flower, and thus it is with our church community . . . . "[5] In the Capeks' original version, the minister actually "consecrated" the vase of flowers. At the end, each individual takes from the vase a different flower from the one that she brought, thus being reminded of the gift that others are to the congregation.

In one sense, the Flower Communion might be deemed a symbolic expression of a more basic sacrament, namely the face-to-face encounter within the community of concrete human beings that provides the plausibility structure for various spiritual paths to show the sacred. Some communicants might, however, experience the sacred itself in the Flower Communion. It is, after all, the contemporary U.U. version of one of humankind's most perennial rituals, the rite of spring. In this regard it ties in with the spiritual focus that finds sacrality in the world of nature. The gathering of the flowers is akin to the old agricultural ritual of gathering the "first fruits" of the harvest, the spring harbingers of all the good that the fecund powers of earth would, the community prayed, bring their way in the months that followed. It turns out, then, that the Flower Communion bridges the gap between contemporary Unitarian Universalist re-enchantment of the world and the enchanted world of ancient peoples, peoples who were ever in touch with the sacred powers of life and growth.

Multi-Dimensional Sacred Space

We shall discover common themes in our analysis of sacred space, sacred time, and sacred language within Unitarian Universalism. First, everyday, non-sacred space, time, and language induce in us the drive to mastery, the drive to make the ego its own controlling deity. But sacred space, time, and language undo the drive to mastery and challenge us to participation and self-transcendence. At the heart of each sort of experience of the sacred we shall discover the by-now familiar fact that we are on a solitary journey *together*. It is only in the context of the larger U.U. community, with its plausibility-conferring function, that the sacred can show itself. At the same time, it is also always a matter of our being on a *solitary* journey together. Thus it is that we shall not encounter in the U.U. community monolithic experiences of sacred space, time, and language. Rather, we shall experience multi-dimensional sacred space, multi-faceted sacred time, and multi-vocative sacred language.

Among the many topics Mircea Eliade has famously explored is that of sacred and profane space. In this instance, however, we shall put Eliade aside and chart a different approach. Let us define ordinary space as space that we can cognitively master. We consistently lay a pragmatic grid over everyday space, dividing it up to suit our purposes: which is the shortest route to my workplace? Which spaces can I use for recreation? In what spaces do I feel at home? What are dangerous spaces that I ought to avoid? The desire to master space has, I would venture, an origin in basic human evolution. Those early hominids who could quickly map the world around them, recalling which areas held danger, which held food and water, and which provided shelter would obviously tend to survive longer and have a better chance of passing on their genetic traits than their fellows who had no such ability to make pragmatic grids. This quest for mastery in the approach to everyday space should not be taken as entirely regrettable. On the contrary, it continues to be crucial for our survival. But might not there also be something more, a different and existentially more fulfilling way of experiencing space?

Sacred space is space experienced as uncanny gift, akin to the ground upon which Moses found himself standing when God appeared to him in the burning bush. Uncanniness is one of the characteristics that Rudolf Otto, who also took a phenomenological approach to religion, attributed to the experience of the sacred—he called it the "Holy"—a characteristic that helps give the sacred its power over us.[6] We do not master sacred space; rather, it masters us. In its presence, we feel the need to remove the sandals of our intellectual presumptuousness.

If the sacred shows itself and the world is re-enchanted in the Unitarian Universalist sanctuary, then the space of the sanctuary is itself sacred. But because the U.U. experience of sacrality is all about pluralism, we must speak of a multi-dimensional sacred space. Let us employ an analogy (it is *only* an analogy) here: one of the most talked-about theories in contemporary physics and cosmology is string theory, which thinks of the fundamental particles and forces that make up the universe in terms of minute vibrating strings. String theory holds that our universe actually has more than the three spatial dimensions that we human beings can perceive. If we were impossibly small beings or had some unimaginably different perceptual equipment, we might see entirely different dimensions of space than those three with which we are in fact familiar. Unitarian Universalists have diverse spiritual foci, and different foci open up different dimensions of sacred space. For example, given your focus on social justice, you might well experience the sacred space of the U.U. sanctuary as a place of justice and peace, set apart from the ordinary world of oppression and struggle. I, by contrast, with my focus upon humanism, might find the sanctuary a temple of self-transcending reason, a place where reason is not distorted by the temptations and contentiousness of the everyday.

We share this sacred space, yet it is variegated, so that the uncanny gift of sacred space shows itself in ways that befit the particular spiritual paths that we pursue.

But U.U. sacred space, while it might show itself in the "sanctuary," is not an escape from the real world. Rather, it is a point of departure, a place in which one encounters the sacred so that one can go back out into the ordinary world recharged with the transformative power of the sacred. Moses did not stay on Mount Sinai after encountering God: he came back down the mountain to lead his people on the basis of what God had revealed to him. Mohammed did not stay in heaven after making his supernatural Night Journey from the Temple Mount in Jerusalem: he returned to his followers in Mecca. So the Unitarian Universalist seeker leaves the multi-dimensional sacred space of the sanctuary to carry on acts of social justice in the world and in order to help re-enchant that larger world, just as the world of the sanctuary has been enchanted.

Multi-Faceted Sacred Time

Ordinary time can be broken up into measurable, equal units. It is what the Greek of the New Testament calls *chronos*, time that, once the age of invention dawns, will be measured by a "chronometer." Despite the imaginative genius that went into Einstein's Special Theory of Relativity, he was admirably succinct and empirical when it came to defining ordinary time: time is what can be measured with a clock. Time, it turns out, is an even more tempting arena for mastery than space. I will always be tempted, within the world of ordinary time, to master my future, to secure purely on my own self-interested terms who I am and what my future shall be, rather than letting the sacred undergird my personhood. John Dominic Crossan goes so far as to equate time-mastery with idolatry, and he avers that Jesus set his message of the Kingdom of God squarely against it.[7]

Human time is all about narration and therefore all about who I am. That is, I create my identity through how I narrate the tale of my life, how I put my life together and interpret it in a story. This is thoroughly tied up with temporality: it is a matter of putting my *memories* in a coherent order, blending them with the *present*, and projecting a *future* in which I shall actualize new dimensions of my selfhood.

But the sacred time that can show itself within the sacred space of the Unitarian Universalist sanctuary undoes the quest for a self-centered mastery of time. This sacred time is not chronological time, but time spent with my fellow questers whose presence midwifes the re-enchantment of the world. This time of re-enchantment is also a time of redemptive re-narration, of being able to project the story of my future in terms not of my own egotistical mastery of time, of an idolatry of time, but in terms of a future that is thoroughly interconnected with the earth and my fellow human beings. My identity is understood as never just that of an isolated subject, but as a matter of being-with. To return to the biblical vocabulary, this sacred time is not *chronos*, but rather *kairos*, "fulfilled time." In some Western traditions there is one all-important *kairos*, a "hinge of history." In Christianity, it is of course the coming of the Christ. In Islam, it is the *hijrah*, the migration by Mohammed and his followers from Mecca to Medina, an event by which the Muslim calendar is oriented. But in the Unitarian Universalist re-enchantment of time, the *kairos*, like sacred space, is not some permanent fixture of reality, but something that is realized in the midst of the community. Furthermore, sacred time for Unitarian Universalists is not uniform; it is multi-faceted, a reflection, as always, of the diversity of U.U. spiritual paths. Thus, for example, for those focused upon nature as the locus of sacrality, to be taken up into sacred time is to be freed from mere chronological time and attuned to nature's time, attuned to the rhythm of the seasons, for example. As a second example, for the quester who focuses on social justice, sacred time is the time in which one is perfectly attuned to the future, but not as the place where her individual ego can be fulfilled. Instead, the devotee of social justice is attuned to the future as *responsibility*, as the time of that which must needs be accomplished. For the follower of the Creative Source/Abyss of the universe, sacred time is experienced, unlike mere chronological time, as the Eternal Now, the extraordinary time in which the meaning and value of the Eternal is present *within* temporality.

Multi-Vocative Sacred Language

Judaism, Christianity, and Islam, the "religions of the book," are text-based traditions. They all claim to possess holy writ through which God/Allah speaks to them. For the most fundamentalist of scriptural interpreters, these sacred texts contain supernaturally revealed duties and supernaturally disclosed facts about God. But the sacredness of word can be understood in a different fashion and can be extended beyond canonical scriptures. Language can be understood as "vocative," from the Latin word which means "to call." Self-transcendence can easily be fit within the experience of language, for language always represents inter-subjectivity, specifically a call from something other than myself.[8] At it most powerful, language calls me outside myself, indeed beyond myself to a new understanding or a new responsibility.

All language has this vocative structure. But then what turns ordinary word into sacred word? In my own particular service of worship in the Unitarian Society of New Haven (Connecticut), I am liable to hear words addressed to me in the form of a Call to Worship, a Meditation, and a Sermon.[9] Does the mere fact that these words take place in the context of a religious service, and perhaps even within sacred space and time, automatically render them sacred ? The answer must surely be "No," for just as most space and most time are secular rather than sacred, so language is most often vocative in a fashion that does not rise to the level of the sacred. There must be some way in which sacred word is especially *pro*-vocative.

For Unitarian Universalists, no language, I would venture, is sacred just in and of itself, not even the world's great Scriptures. This follows from the U.U. rejection of any unchallangable religious authority, whether it be person, text, creed, or tradition. It seems, then, that language *becomes* sacred language for certain persons in particular circumstances. One must be properly attuned at the moment of receiving the words being spoken or read; one must have Jesus' "ears to hear." After all, words too can be mere instruments of mastery. All of our concepts are borne by words—from "dog," to "person," to "love." It is no accident that philosophers traditionally called concepts *universals*. The concept "dog" is universal, because we can place under it all dogs in all times and places, all dogs that we shall ever encounter. Words, then, provide us with a potent conceptual mastery indeed! Even here language is vocative: the concept "dog" calls me, invites me, to grasp the character of the furry four-legged creature that I see running through the park chasing a ball. There is even a weak, non-challenging inter-subjectivity involved here: the concept "dog" puts me in touch with how my language tradition has chosen to categorize the world and the things and beings that make it up.

But as we well know by now, there is something special about how I encounter reality amongst my fellows within the Unitarian Universalist community of devotion. When I am face to face with a community of fellow human beings who, precisely insofar as they are with me on a spiritual search, confront me with the seriousness and potential sacredness of the whole human project, then the language addressed to me can become fully *pro*-vocative. For, as part of the questing community, I am not allowed the luxury of understanding the vocative character of language as simply a formal feature of words, a feature that can be reduced to the fact that language serves as a medium of information exchange. Instead, language becomes a concrete and personal address from these flesh-and-blood others. And the especially potent otherness represented by the variegated U.U. community and the diversity of its members' quests only ups the ante: any notion that I have mastered the world through language is exploded by the many worldviews different from my own held by those who sit around me in the sanctuary. Hence, I know that the words uttered by the minister in the midst of the service cannot be simply taken up into my arsenal of words for mastering my environment. Rather, those words are genuinely provocative for me, they are made to reveal new, unthought of, sacred meaning just insofar as I share my hearing of them with others who will interpret them through different lenses and in whom they will touch different experiences. Now I am truly addressed by something beyond my control. Language is no mere tool: it is a call to participation and self-transcendence. Mere word has become multi-vocative sacred word.

When I read the minister's sermon as posted on the church's website a week after the service in which it was actually preached, the words of the sermon may or may not have the same effect upon me. It will depend upon whether I read the sermon in splendid isolation, or if, even though I am sitting at home alone in front of my computer, I read it thinking of myself as participating in the identity-and-difference of the congregation and, ultimately, of the larger universe. No word is sacred just in and of itself. It *becomes* sacred, *becomes* provocative in the proper circumstances.

By way of conclusion to our explorations in this chapter, let us think back to poor Lisa Simpson's empty bowl in Chapter

One. We decided there that the U.U. chalice is in fact empty, but in the ultimately productive sense that it is empty of congealed ideologies and prohibitive theological dogmas. Hence, the chalice can be filled by the fuel of diverse spiritual quests. Many quests, one chalice. We are on a solitary journey together in Unitarian Universalism, and we now have a bit more concrete notion of how that unique quest re-enchants and re-sacralizes the world and its most basic elements.

Notes for Chapter Three

[1] Gerard Manley Hopkins, "Inversnaid," in *Poems and Prose*, ed. W.H. Gardner (New York: Penguin, 1978), p. 50.

[2] *www.uua.org/aboutuu/flowercommunion*, April 1, 2004.

[3] Rosemary Radford Ruether, *Sexism and God-Talk: Toward a Feminist Theology* (Boston: Beacon, 1983), p. 138.

[4] Ralph Waldo Emerson, "Divinity School Address," in Parke, ed., *The Epic of Unitarianism*, pp. 105-110.

[5] www.uua.org/aboutuu/flowercommunion

[6] See Rudolf Otto, *The Idea of the Holy*, trans. John W. Harvey (London: Oxford University, 1923).

[7] Crossan, *In Parables*, p. 27.

[8] My own words that I wrote in my journal yesterday are still from an "I" who occupies a different point in time than the "I" who reads the journal entry today. Hence, those words can still call to me, not only in the sense of reminding me of things that I have forgotten, but even in the sense of disclosing something to me that I was not aware of when I actually wrote the words. It is also worth noting here that the vocative character of language can be understood in both a more traditional and a more postmodernist sense. In the more traditional approach, what addresses me in spoken language or the language of a text is the author of the words. From the postmodern perspective, by contrast, language, especially in its textual form, is set free from the intentions of its author, but that in

no way limits the ability of language to address, question, and empower me.

[9] Note that *"Call* to Worship" is an expression foregrounding the vocative character of language.

Chapter Four

A Contrarian Interlude

A particular argument is no stronger than its ability to ward off the most obvious objections that can be raised against it. Thus, it is desirable to consider such possible objections and to deactivate them in advance, saving one's intellectual opponents the trouble of making the objections in the first place. I have been arguing that the unique dynamic of identity-in-difference that characterizes Unitarian Universalism can re-enchant the world. In the first part of what follows, I shall put forward what seem to me to be potentially strong objections to this claim; I shall attempt to present the objections as powerfully as possible. In the latter part of the chapter, I shall consider how the objections might be countered.

The present chapter is indeed an interlude, a term that we derive from the Latin *ludes*, which means "play." We shall consider the *interplay*, the back and forth (what philosophers call the "dialectic") of argument and counter-argument here. But the word "interlude" also suggests a break in the action. This second meaning applies too, insofar as the basic argument of the book will be interrupted by a consideration of what might count against it. This interruption will take up the most technical—some might say the most "hairsplitting"—topics to be treated in the book, and as an interruption, it can be skipped by readers who do not wish to be sidetracked by what they may well regard as unnecessary technicalities. One should, thus, feel free to move on to Chapter Five at this point, if he or she wishes to do so.

Objection One: Suppose that Fred believes that the spiritual fulfillment of the human race is not to be found in something such as a transcendent God nor in identification with nature and the universe. Rather, Fred is convinced that there exists a race of extraterrestrials that is vastly superior to earthlings, both intellectually and spiritually. What is more, Fred believes that, if one properly attunes oneself telepathically to these extraterrestrials, which one can do via a form of meditation that he has discovered, they will one day swoop down in their spaceship and whisk one away to a life of spiritual fulfillment. Now it is more than likely that most of Fred's friends, family members, and acquaintances do not share his enthusiasm for such extraterrestrial spiritual pursuits. His belief thus lacks inter-subjective validity. It has no socially-provided plausibility structure. As a result, he may hold it with a measure of suppressed doubt. Indeed, his conviction may become the form of fanaticism associated with a split consciousness—belief stands over against repressed doubt—which results in the need to protest too much, to trumpet his belief so loudly that it drowns out his unbelief.

Ah, but relief from Fred's predicament is on the way! One day, a friend takes Fred with her to visit her local Unitarian Universalist church. Fred is immediately attracted to what he sees there, and he soon joins. Now his spiritual vision is given inter-subjective validity and a social plausibility structure. In other words, his belief is given what would appear to be a healthy, functional sort of reinforcement, overcoming his split religious consciousness and the resultant need to protest too much. Note that his newly discovered U.U. companions need not share the particular content of his spirituality. Indeed, there may not be a single one of them who buys into his expectation of a high-tech trip across the final frontier. But they nonetheless give his vision inter-subjective validity just insofar as they affirm all individuals and their quests, however idiosyncratic, as long as those quests do not violate the U.U. Principles.

How does this scenario constitute an objection to my argument in this book? After all, Fred's spiritual vision does receive inter-subjective validity. The problem, of course, is that we may be conferring inter-subjective validity upon something that every other member of the church in question considers "wacko." Be entirely honest: how do you picture Fred, not physically (though that could enter the equation), but psychologically and socially? Do you imagine him as outgoing and gregarious, as a person whom everyone at the office seeks out for conversation, as a favorite lunch companion? Do you regard him as the first person in whom you should confide if you are experiencing significant problems? My guess is that you do not. Instead, you assume that someone whose ultimate concern has to do with telepathic contact with space aliens is not socially adjusted in an entirely healthy fashion. It is possible, then, that no other member of Fred's church considers his spiritual vision a healthy one. Doesn't this example make it evident, then, that the dynamic of U.U. identity and difference that provides a social plausibility structure for each seeker's quest is dangerously indiscriminate? It can just as well add fuel to wholly illusory, even hallucinatory, fires as to real ones. Perhaps this is not such a happy dynamic after all.

Objection Two: This objection is closely related to the first. Many U.U. paths are not *directly* connected with truth claims. Rather, they are about particular spiritual practices, such as Buddhist meditation, or attempting to live the kind of simple lifestyle that does not harm the earth.[1] Some paths do, however, put truth claims in the foreground, so that, even if a particular path can be called a spiritual practice, it is a practice that is being used in large measure as an avenue to setting forth a cognitive claim. The pathway envisioned by our outer-space-infatuated friend above is an example of one that seems to have a particular set of cognitive claims as an essential part of its identity. Or perhaps what makes it notable is that it rests on cognitive claims that would be widely disputed, whereas the cognitive claims indirectly set forth or presupposed by many U.U. quests—for example, that yoga is good for you—are not particularly controversial. Fred holds that there are super-superior extraterrestrial beings with whom he is in telepathic contact. Most persons will not accept this claim. Indeed, let us once again attempt total honesty. If this space(y) spirituality were revealed to me by its ardent devotee, I might quite seriously suggest the he consult the church's minister and take advantage of a bit of free psychological counseling. She might, in turn, be tempted to refer Fred to a psychiatrist, who could attempt some pharmacological neurotransmitter re-calibration.

The first objection suggested that the U.U. dynamic at the heart of this book may indiscriminately confer plausibility upon any old spirituality, whether healthy or destructive. This second objection teases out a slightly different possibility: maybe the dynamic does not in fact confer plausibility on *all* spiritual quests (even if they do cohere with the U.U. Principles). Some quests depend more than others on particular truth claims. For those truth claims to receive plausibility, they must have inter-subjective validity. But truth claims, unlike some other sorts of human activity—meditating, writing poetry, helping the poor—can sometimes contradict one another. And there are some truth claims that already have inter-subjective validity and are nearly universally held in our U.U. community before Fred becomes a member. Such truth claims include the following: the earth is (roughly) spherical; the universe has existed for more than five minutes; and, unfortunately for Fred, persons who look to space aliens to whisk them away to salvation inevitably display various difficulties in dealing with life.

In summary of objection two, it turns out that not all spiritual quests, especially those that foreground particular truth claims, are granted inter-subjective validity by the U.U. community and hence a plausibility structure. And this means, furthermore, that the world is not re-enchanted via just every path pursued by members of the U.U. community. But this opens the proverbial can of worms, for now we are faced with all kinds of questions about just which quests will be affirmed and on what grounds.

Objection Three: If the first objection suggested that the blessing of all quests by our U.U. dynamic leads to a dangerously indiscriminate bestowal of reality, and the second objection raised the possibility that not all of the contents of all spiritual quests pursued within our community are in fact given a plausibility structure, the third objection goes farther and holds that the affirmation of diverse quests does not really affirm the *content* of any of those quests. Rather, it only affirms the individual quester's right to pursue whatever content he or she finds meaningful (assuming that it does not violate the Principles). That is, the underlying common structure of participation and self-transcendence is affirmed along with one's right to fill in the content as she sees fit. The content, it turns out, is essentially indifferent as far as the conferral of plausibility is concerned. One way to look at it would be to say that Fred is back in business now: he is free to fill in the structure of participation and self-transcendence with the notion that he participates in the wisdom of superior beings from beyond the earth. But another, perhaps more accurate, way to see it is to say that we are all *out* of business: while our spiritual attempts, just *qua* attempts, are granted inter-subjective validity (which, note, they would still lack in dogmatic traditions that prescribe a single way) and hence the aura of reality, the content of each attempt is untouched by this process. The content of my particular spiritual way is left hanging; it is a blind leap. But if my faith is mere blind leap with no social plausibility conferred upon it, what has the U.U. community added? Wouldn't I be just as well off sitting alone in my living room practicing a ritual known only to me? Isn't the New Age, which has no institutional connections of note—except the engine of capitalism that powers it to a much larger degree than often noticed—just as well off all by itself without anything like the Unitarian Universalist community?

Rejoinder: The three objections that we have just considered, most especially the third, threaten the whole enterprise of this book. If the content of our spiritual quests is not affirmed by our fellow U.U. questers, then the magic of re-enchantment cannot occur. Now, as it turns out, I agree with one of the implications of the objections. The objections remind us, rightly I think, that not *all* worldviews are affirmed by Unitarian Universalism. My eighth-grade Affirmations students are fond of informing me and my co-teachers that they like Unitarian Universalism because "You can believe anything that you want." That, of course, is stretching the liberalism of liberal religion too far. As already indicated, a spiritual program that clearly violates the U.U. Principles will not be affirmed. I cannot be a Nazi and, at the same time, a member in good standing of the U.U. faith community.

But there is another, deeper level to the objections, and that is the suggestion that the U.U. community will also refuse to endorse some spiritual quests even if those quests do not in fact violate the Principles. The suggestion is that there may be, in some instances, a clash of truth claims that nixes the process of conferring inter-subjective validity, the process that supposedly ultimately leads to re-enchantment. Members of Fred's U.U. church are, for example, nearly unanimous in holding the truth claims that the earth is spherical, that the universe has existed for more than five minutes, and that persons religiously fixated on their contacts with the crews of interstellar vessels are in a psychologically unhealthy state. Hence, given Fred's claims and their contradiction of the general convictions of the community, Fred's quest will not be affirmed by that community.

This possibility that some quests are left out of the process through which social plausibility is conferred led to the even more severe suggestion that what actually occurs in the U.U. dynamic at the heart of our exploration is that the *content* of our quests is never affirmed, at least not necessarily, by our fellow questers. I have my quest and you have yours, and their contents contradict one another. What is affirmed by the whole U.U. community in this scenario is just the common underlying structure of participation and self-transcendence along with my right—assuming harmony with the Principles—to fill in the content of the structure as I see fit. But this hardly seems sufficient to re-enchant the world. It is the content of my spiritual way, after all, upon which I focus and through which I hope to make contact with the sacred. If it is not given the aura of reality, then the main argument of this book is simply false.

But now it is time to unpack the objections a bit more carefully and show where, it seems to me, they go wrong. Suppose that I am a theist: I believe that there exists a personal Supreme Being who has created the heavens and the earth. However, I do not believe that any particular religious tradition has a monopoly on the truth about God or fully grasps God's reality. Hence, I choose to practice my theism within the Unitarian Universalist community. Angelica, by contrast, is an old-fashioned, hard-nosed humanist. She is certain that no God exists (while neither the existence nor the nonexistence of God can be proven with mathematical rigor, one can still be certain of one's beliefs about God, given that certainty is a matter of a *decision* that I make about what I believe, rather than something just inherent in evidence or lack of it). Clearly there are truth claims involved in our differing spiritual paths, truth claims that just as clearly flatly contradict one another. This should mean, according to the objections considered above, that I cannot affirm Angelica's path, nor she mine. And, of course, it is this kind of scenario that raises the possibility that the affirmation of one another's paths within Unitarian Universalist communities is never, in fact, an affirmation of the content of those paths.

But the crucial fact of the matter is that I will happily affirm Angelica's path, and she will happily affirm mine, and those affirmations will include content, despite the obvious competing truth claims involved here. Angelica will support my embrace of theism because she knows that different persons see the world differently and, hence, require different sorts of spiritual approaches. What is more, though she firmly rejects theism in her own mind, she gives me the benefit of the doubt and believes that my theism is put forward in good faith, that I have had life experiences that provide what I consider a firm basis for my theistic convictions. My theism has integrity in her mind, it is authentic, and thus she can happily affirm it as one more quest within the U.U. community. And, of course, I approach her religious humanism in the same spirit. Humanism is not for me, but I assume, unless shown otherwise, that Angelica too has her reasons for embracing humanism and that they make humanism a perfectly reasonable choice for her. We confer our blessing on one another's spiritual ways.

It turns out, then, that Fred's case was misleading. It appeared that Fred's project was denied social plausibility within the community because of a clash of truth claims: other people in the church did not believe in telepathically-available space aliens. But the bare clash of truth claims is not enough to cause difficulty, as we see in the relationship between my theism and Angelica's humanism. The larger community did indeed reject Fred's claims, but what they were rejecting was not those truth claims as such, i.e., in isolation from their larger use and effects. The reality of the matter is that the community, rightly or wrongly, associated Fred's constellation of truth claims with a psychologically dysfunctional lifestyle. *That* is the problem. I have no particular reason to reject out of hand the possibility of intelligent extraterrestrial life, even life that has its own way of making contact with earth dwellers. And even if I did reject this notion, I could affirm someone else's belief in such beings, just insofar as the issue is one of a bare truth claim. But in this case, the bare truth claims are connected in the minds of the majority of contemporary Americans, including those who signed the membership book of Fred's Unitarian Universalist church, with the fear that a religious fervor about such beliefs inevitably leads to maladjustment. Not for nothing did Fred's co-seekers deem Fred, admittedly with a decided lack of U.U. compassion, a "wacko."

I contend, then, that we are back in business, having uncovered the confusions that power the three objections. Members of the Unitarian Universalist community do in fact affirm one another's spiritual projects, including the content of those projects, even when the truth claims in others' projects conflict with one's own. Only those projects are left out that violate the U.U. Principles or that seem to lead to what the community deems an unhealthy lifestyle. And, of course, these two limiting elements are connected: one can easily argue, for example, that the Principles' articulation of a commitment to human dignity rules out supporting others on paths that lead, by the lights of the Principles, to a truncated existence, for if one were to affirm such paths, one would be party to denying a fellow quester the full humanity that is due him or her. In conclusion, if we cannot go quite so far as naively to exult that "God's in his heaven and all's right with the world," we *can* say that the world is safe for re-enchantment.

Notes for Chapter Four

[1] Spiritual practices do not focus on truth claims; they are not themselves primarily assertions, but they of course rest on certain implied truth claims. For example, practicing Buddhist meditation

presumably rests on the assumption that meditation is good for me. One of the ways in which this sort of practice can be seen to assert truth claims only indirectly is that quite different, even contradictory claims—metaphysical claims about what is ultimately real, for example—could equally well support the spiritual practice in question. Different metaphysical worldviews could explain, for instance, why Buddhist meditation is good for me.

Chapter Five

Why Are We Here?

The focus of our explorations thus far has been on how the Unitarian Universalist community re-enchants the world for its members. Drawing on the common spiritual dynamic of participation and self-transcendence, expressing that dynamic in many forms, and then bringing those forms together in a mutually supportive community that lends each quest social plausibility and hence the aura of reality, the Unitarian Universalist experience reacquaints us with Mystery and the sacred. The cosmos, and our daily lives, are re-enchanted. Understanding this scenario has required a brush with the discipline called sociology of religion. We have put a good deal of weight, for example, on sociologist Peter Berger's notion of the social plausibility structure. For the most part, however, we have concentrated on the social dynamics *within* the U.U. community. We know what Unitarian Universalism accomplishes . . . for its own members. Now it is time to step back and ask how Unitarian Universalism fits within the larger milieu of North American religiosity and spirituality. Why are we here, as Unitarian Universalist communities? What, in particular, do we have to contribute to the larger religious and social scene in North America and beyond?

In order to answer this question, it is helpful to look at four basic patterns of religion in a society. While some of the four will be more descriptive of times long past than of the present, each will, in its own way, help illuminate the particular pattern that Unitarian Universalism confronts in contemporary North American society. The patterns will help locate us. Each of these patterns is an "ideal type," meant to emphasize certain fundamental dynamics at work in a society's relationship to religion and spirituality. In real life, things are always messier than ideal types let on, but the types are useful for purposes of highlighting and clarifying the most important dynamics at work.

The first pattern, which we shall call **Christendom**, is in many ways the simplest. It is the scenario in which one religious tradition permeates a whole society so that the society is spiritually monolithic rather than pluralistic. Something roughly akin to Christendom most likely held sway in simple tribal cultures and in most preliterate societies. Christendom proper, however, begins with the conversion of the Roman Emperor Constantine to Christianity in the fourth century of the Common Era. Christianity soon became the official, authoritative religion of the Roman Empire, spread by the Roman armies as they marched hither and yon throughout Europe. It was in this period that Christian worship and the vestments of Christian clerics began to mimic the pomp and circumstance of the imperial court.

But Christendom in its purest and most potent form came to birth in Western European society in the Middle Ages. The term "Christendom" finds its literal application here—the Christian kingdom—because the Christian church dominated the entire culture, informing not only spirituality, but morality, aesthetics, and even economics. The Church forbade "usury," for instance, that is, the charging of interest rates on loans (something contemporary capitalism would be hard-pressed to do without). Of course Jews also lived in Western Europe during the Middle Ages. They were, to put it mildly, a persecuted minority. Subject to pogroms and expulsions and inquisitions, blamed for everything from the Black Plague to carting off Christian children and draining their blood to make matzah, Jews at various point were ghettoized in the most literal sense: they were forced to live in a walled-off section of the city, the gates of the ghetto being locked at night. Hitler's Holocaust could never have taken place without the long history of European Christian anti-Judaism and anti-Semitism. But life in the ghetto, from a purely socio-religious point of view, provided its own kind of monolithic experience. That is, there too there was one unchallenged religious tradition, whatever its subdivisions. The Middle Ages in Western Europe, then, were characterized by the virtual absence of religious pluralism. While this monolithic socio-religious scenario has a vastly important place in Western history and culture, it is not exactly the situation in which we currently find ourselves in contemporary North America, *though we shall see that it does live on, in a mutant form, when we look at the fourth ideal type below, the type that comes closest to characterizing our own society today.*

Furthermore, we can connect Christendom and its monolithic, intolerant attitude, with the birth of Unitarian Universalism. The lockstep theology of the Middle Ages surely created a powerful sense of claustrophobia and constriction, especially among spiritually and intellectually gifted seekers. That sense finally exploded with full force in the Protestant Reformation of the sixteenth century. While a great many spiritually and theologically creative individuals obviously remained within the Roman Catholic fold, the Reformation did begin the freeing-up of Western Christianity. While, as has been noted earlier, unitarian and universalist sympathies can be found in at least nascent form in the Reformation period itself, they came to their own later on. The Calvinist tradition produced much of the theology and practice that made up New England Congregationalism. Despite the impeccable Reformation credentials of Calvinism, the New England Puritan colonies informed by it, such as the Massachusetts Bay Colony and the New Haven Colony, were hardly gardens of spiritual freedom and experimentation. American unitarianism and universalism are related to the monolithic character of Christendom, then, in that it is the very rejection of that monolithic attitude that gave unitarianism and universalism much of their reason for being.

Our second ideal social type, while it may be at the opposite extreme from Christendom in terms of its belief content, actually presents a similarly monolithic situation, namely, an unchallenged **secularism**. Here the ideality of the ideal type is more in evidence: it is not clear that we can find any example of a culture that is monolithically secular. However, as was indicated in the Introduction, parts of Europe, perhaps especially the Scandinavian countries, appear to be more and more secular all of the time. Now this secularism has nothing at all to do with the bogeyman of Christian fundamentalism that Jerry Fallwell and others call "secular humanism." Fallwell and his ilk try to convince us that there is some organized movement with characteristic tenets called secular humanism, and that it is self-consciously taught in our public schools. Nothing could be farther from reality.

The truly secular woman or man, far from bandying about a menacing arsenal of anti-religious shibboleths, simply never thinks about religion or spirituality at all. It never enters her mind. Compare the agnostic, or even the reluctant atheist, who cares enough about God to contemplate God's death, even if the sense of God's absence is deflected by humor, as in Woody Allen's observation that "God is not dead, he's just an underachiever."

What does someone do with her life if she never, ever brings to mind questions of Mystery, spirituality, and transcendence? If she is a resident of the twenty-first century West, then the path of least resistance—there may be other, healthier paths of course—is to allow her wants and values to be formed by the dictates of multinational capitalism. I am what I desire to own; I am what I wear and what I drive; I am the body that I display through the camouflage of the latest moisturizers and makeup and even through the latest form of plastic surgery. I may still be a being related to a larger world, a being-in-the-world and a being-with-others. But as Marxist theorists will observe, if there are any of them left out there, all of the entities and even all of the persons in my world, including myself, have now been reduced to commodities.

We might speak, metaphorically and mythically, of two Falls, remembering that while metaphors and myths should not be taken literally, they can bring into view profound truths about our condition. As this myth opens, human beings have the highest possible dignity. They are children of God who find themselves in the direct presence of God in the Garden of Eden. But then they opt egotistically for mastery, not just over against God but also over against their fellows. They fall, and their dignity is reduced a notch: they are still children of God, but now they live in a state of estrangement from God. But at some point in human history, a point that constitutes an even more devastating Fall, human beings lose even the dignity that belongs to an estranged child of God, for they are no longer spiritual beings at all, but simply commodities, the products of powerful market forces.

Part of what sociologists mean by a secular society is a society in which religion no longer plays the central, unifying role that it once did but is replaced by the economy. It is the economy that holds the society together and provides its rules. But the problem is that economic rules are not values, they are simply dicta of economic efficiency. While we do not live in a purely secular society, one that conforms to our ideal type, secularity is nonetheless a potent current within the world that we inhabit. If an examination of Christendom gave us some sense of where we come from, the examination of secularity begins to give us resources for answering the question, "Why are we U.U.s here?" "What is our place in the contemporary world?" For surely part of our role is to oppose the commodification of human beings and the world, to hold high the banner of human dignity in the face of one of the most powerful dehumanizing dynamics that the world has ever seen.

The Unitarian Universalist opposition to a thoroughgoing secularization will look nothing like the Christian fundamentalist opposition to "secular humanism." On the surface, it might appear as if the two camps could make common cause here. Christian fundamentalists certainly condemn pornography, for instance, and pornography is an example of the sort of commodification of human beings that I have been condemning above. But something like pornography is not the disease itself, but only one of its symptoms (one ought not to forget, of course, that symptoms are themselves often highly destructive). While Christian fundamentalism may joust against a symptom such as pornography, the larger picture reveals that American fundamentalists are thoroughly captive to runaway capitalism. This is frighteningly evident, for example, in how the fundamentalists so thoroughly identify themselves with American militarism and its protection of everything from American fruit companies that operate south of our borders to foreign oil fields that supply the lifeblood of a plethora of Western oil companies. While we would be wholly remiss were we to suppose that all Christian conservatives are cut from exactly the same cloth— there are social-justice Evangelicals, for example—it is nonetheless rare to find an American Christian fundamentalist who would not embrace the slogan "My country, right or wrong." And that country today, despite its being a frightening, imperialistic superpower, does not, as it turns out, represent a thoroughly independent entity. Now, it is certainly true that nationalism can be a destructive, idolatrous enterprise, as Washington "neo-cons" have made all too evident. But the America of today is ultimately not a discrete entity, however powerful its military, but rather the "biggest, baddest" piece of the multinational capitalist puzzle.

I leave it to others to determine whether one of the reasons why we Unitarian Universalists need to be on the scene today is to oppose multinational capitalism *as such*, or whether the challenge is to fight a particular *perversion* of what capitalism can be. But one way or another, as our U.U. Principles make clear, we are surely here to fight for human dignity and thus to oppose forces such as those that precipitate the human race's Second Fall, that destroy our dignity by making us mere articles of consumption.

Given what we have seen in our first three chapters, we ought to keep one reason, in particular, in mind when contemplating U.U. convictions about human dignity. Traditional Judaism and

Christianity would say that persons have dignity and worth because they were created in the image of God. Some U.U.s might agree. But, if our foregoing analysis is sound, all members of the Unitarian Universalist community ought to be able to defend human dignity on the basis of the human ability to participate in the sacred and to reach out to Mystery. We are not mere "its," mere items that possess "exchange value." On the contrary, we are self-transcending beings who can inhabit an enchanted cosmos, a cosmos that is, precisely as enchanted, redolent with meaning, value, and purpose. Human beings are animals to which the Holy shows itself![1]

The third ideal type of a relationship between religion and society is what we shall call **inclusive pluralism**. We find a clear example of inclusive pluralism among the Ancient Greeks. Greek religion operated on multiple levels, and a single individual could participate at each level. For example, there were rites performed at a family altar. There were sacrifices and rituals that were the provenance of an entire city. There were rituals on behalf of the Greeks as a whole (the famous games at Olympia, for example, centered around sacrifice to a god). In addition to all of this, in the later part of Ancient Greek history, an individual Greek might well choose to join one of many different "mystery religions," so called because they involved secret initiations and the transmission of mysteries, mysteries often tied to a successful journey through the underworld after death. One might join a mystery cult dedicated to Dionysus, or Demeter, or Mithras.[2] This is an "inclusive pluralism," then, because it is constituted by many religious sites and practices, but an individual can happily participate in any number of them. He or she is not forced to pick just one religion out of the pluralistic milieu and embrace it as his or her sole spiritual path.

We find a similar pattern even today in many Asian societies. In Japan, for instance, as has often been observed, one can have a Shinto wedding and a Buddhist funeral. There is no sense of religions being wholly discrete institutional entities whose boundaries prevent participation in more than one religion at a time. It is probably Wilfred Cantwell Smith who has had the most impact of any one scholar on contemporary understanding of how our notion of "a religion" developed. The idea that a religion is a definitely bounded entity is a relatively recent Western invention according to Smith. It leads us into the error, he suggests, of supposing that something called "a religion" can, in and of itself, be true or false, when those categories should properly be reserved for ways in which actual human individuals choose to live their lives. "A religion" can no more be true than can a culture.[3] But what a particular spiritual tradition provides an individual can be employed by that individual in such a way that she lives ethically, morally, "truly."

Is inclusive pluralism necessarily equivalent to polytheism? The Ancient Greeks, of course, are usually regarded as polytheists. Suppose that I imagine an inclusive pluralism wherein the various objects of devotion are not personified but are values or powers or facets of the natural world. Then the spirituality spawned by inclusive pluralism will not be poly-*theism* in the technical sense. But what of its effects? Sometimes it is claimed that having a single ultimate concern or object of devotion, such as is the case in Judaism, Christianity, and Islam, is pragmatically desirable (bracketing any questions about metaphysical truth). The argument is that, for the self to be secure and reasonably unified, it must have a single focus for its devotion. Consider, by contrast, the poor Greek polytheists: they honored one god at the risk of offending another; they felt compelled to scurry mindlessly from one temple to another, never having a single center of gravity for their life paths.

But if we are not talking about actual gods and goddesses, about anthropomorphic beings who can't resist insinuating themselves at the most inopportune times into human affairs, then is this concern really valid? Might not multiple objects of devotion and value actually enrich the seeker, making him or her spiritually more dexterous and able to take advantage of a much wider array of spiritual resources?

Alternatively, couldn't one read an inclusive pluralism in a way that does not abandon the notion of underlying unity? The sacred shows itself in many ways; the Mysterious Depth is visible from many spiritual vantage points. But it is the same sacred, the same Mysterious Depth that is making itself known in each instance. This is what Hindu philosophers say, after all, when they juxtapose the idea of Brahman, the all-encompassing Godhead, with Indians' devotion to a plethora of gods and goddesses from Krishna to Kali. The one, infinite Godhead has many incarnations, each an "avatar" that can connect with particular persons in particular circumstances.

In any case, our own society today cannot be put under the heading of inclusive pluralism. Rather, it comes closest to our final ideal type, **exclusive pluralism**. That expression may appear to be an oxymoron. If a religious situation is pluralistic, how can it also be exclusive? Recall our discussion above about how the West has conceived of religions as discrete entities with nearly impenetrable institutional boundaries. Contemporary North American society is certainly religiously pluralistic: there are almost too many religious options to count. But we are expected to pick *one* of them. If it turns out that I was married as a Methodist and cremated as a Buddhist, then people will say that, at some point in my life, I "converted." One cannot serve two—or three or four—masters.

We have already come upon one significant response to the question, "Why are we here?" We are here to champion the dignity of the human person over against the dehumanizing forces of commodification. We are here to celebrate the human being's ability to discern the sacred and to stand, awestruck, before Mystery. But now we can add another answer to the question of why U.U.s are here, an answer that is perhaps not as immediately obvious as the first answer. Is it not increasingly our unique contribution to present to our society the possibility of an inclusive pluralism? We are ourselves inclusively pluralistic as a community, but wouldn't it be desirable for us to model that inclusive pluralism in such an attractive and compelling fashion that it becomes not simply an option within but also without? In other words, wouldn't it be the healthiest and richest of all possible spiritual worlds if our society as a whole were inclusively pluralistic as opposed to exclusively pluralistic? This is not the same as saying that all traditions should become Unitarian Universalism. Not at all. Conservative Judaism, for example, would not become indistinguishable from Buddhism, such that they would both simply pull together whatever spiritual resources happened to be in the air at the time. On the contrary, Buddhism would stay Buddhism and Conservative Judaism would stay Conservative Judaism, but my neighbors would no longer be taken aback if I were to tell them that I was a Conservative Jew and a Buddhist.

This seems to me one of the most exciting possible answers to the question "Why are we here?" At the same time, it may appear overly optimistic, if not downright naive. Can we really envision such a radical change in North American piety, and is it reasonable to suppose that Unitarian Universalism could actually have a significant impact on any movement toward such a change? I choose to take the positive, hopeful view on these matters, and in defense of my optimism I refer back to the larger, long-term dynamics of Western culture. Secularization, which does its unintentional best to dismantle traditional religious configurations, continues apace in our society. Indeed, like the expansion of the physical universe, it is probably accelerating, as multi-national capitalism grows exponentially. Given this course of events, hermetically sealed religious institutions will be even less tenable, if possible at all, two hundred years from now. Why not, then, an inclusive pluralism, helped along to a not insignificant degree by the example of Unitarian Universalism? There are good reasons for us to be here. The future, in particular, promises a world in which our contributions can be particularly significant.

Notes to Chapter Five

[1]   Whether there is a sense in which the sacred shows itself to other members of the animal kingdom is, without doubt, a fascinating (and perhaps important) question. I feel reasonably confident in saying that some Unitarian Universalists would assert that other animals do indeed, in their own ways, experience the Holy.

[2]   For a description of how religion operated at multiple levels of Greek society, as well as the characteristics of the mystery religions, see Walter Burkert, *Greek Religion*, trans. John Raffan (Cambridge: Harvard University, 1987).

[3]   See Wilfred Cantwell Smith, *The Meaning and End of Religion* (Minneapolis: Augsburg Fortress, 1994).

Chapter Six

Epilogue: Divining the Future

In the first chapter of this book, I set forth a weighty claim on behalf of Unitarian Universalism. The world around us has become ever more secularized, ever more disenchanted. Mystery and sacrality seem to be in eclipse. As traditional institutional religions slowly wither, however, individual seekers are making innumerable attempts to connect with the sacred, but their lone efforts often bear little fruit. Unless my spiritual worldview is reinforced by other persons, unless it possesses inter-subjective validity, it will not seem fully real to me. Unitarian Universalism accomplishes the extraordinary task for its members of re-enchanting the world: by bringing sundry individual quests together within a single community where the whole body of seekers affirms the quest of each member, and the requisite inter-subjective validity is provided. A social plausibility structure is built under our quests, so that we can experience re-enchantment and Mystery.

If the first Four chapters of the book set forth a weighty claim about what Unitarian Universalism can achieve for its members, Chapter Five has set forth an equally weighty and ambitious claim about what Unitarian Universalism might accomplish for the world at large, or at least for our culture. What are the actual prospects for this vision? Can we divine the future of Unitarian Universalism in North American society? The expression "to divine the future" invites a pun, of course: can we help our society uncover the "divine," the sacred, the Mysterious Depth? Does the North American future really contain the possibility of re-enchantment accomplished, in part at least, through the mediation of Unitarian Universalism?

Thomas Jefferson famously opined that every young man (*sic*) alive in Jefferson's own time would die a Unitarian. His prediction was slightly off-target. One thing we can learn from Jefferson's enthusiastic misjudgment is modesty, obviously. But, perhaps more important, we can learn patience and a sense of the time-scale involved in massive social change. Jefferson was a paradigmatic example of an Enlightenment thinker. The Enlightenment was that movement in eighteenth-century European intellectual circles that championed reason in all things (a narrowly construed, Western, white male reading of reason, to be sure). We see his Enlightenment commitments in the words of the *Declaration of Independence*: "We hold these truths to be *self-evident* . . . . [italics added] And we see them in his abridgment of the Gospels, the *Jefferson Bible* with which so many U.U.s are familiar, in which he removes any hint of the supernatural and focuses on the rational and ethical in the teaching of Jesus.

But the Enlightenment, which must have looked to Jefferson as if it would inevitably permeate Western culture in but a few decades time, ended up meeting unexpected resistance. Some of the most talented artists and thinkers of the nineteenth century found Enlightenment rationality cold and uninspiring, hence one motive for the launch of the Romantic movement. And sociologist Max Weber, who coined the phrase "disenchantment of the world" to describe secularization, saw the Enlightenment leading to our imprisonment in an "iron cage." Since that time, many more thinkers have added their complaints about the Enlightenment. It is a particularly heinous villain in most postmodern visions of history. Most thinkers, it seems, have written off the Enlightenment.[1] And, as a result, they have sometimes written off Jefferson's Enlightenment attitude about the inevitable liberalization of religion.

But the dictum that comes to mind here is "Not so fast!" The story is not finished yet. While the specific notion of reasonableness and liberality that Jefferson found in the Enlightenment may have been fatally flawed, the larger vision of a culture in which religious liberalism triumphs may yet be valid. After all, we have all along been operating with the well-documented assumption that traditional religion is slowly wilting on the vine, and that quite different forms of spirituality are struggling to take its place. We need to take the *long* view. The religious trajectory of Western society from the seventeenth century into the future will, I would argue, eventually result in either a thoroughgoing secularism—monolithic secularism, in the language of the previous chapter—or in liberal spiritualities. It is the facts of secularization that make this two-fold possibility by far the most likely future scenario. And this means, of course, that the prospects for Unitarian Universalism surviving and even helping to midwife the re-enchantment of the larger culture are bright.

Of course, these happy prospects must be vigorously grasped. Recall James Luther Adams' injunctions about the need for action and the duty to avoid the naive assumption that things inevitably turn out well all of their own accord. If the future of first world societies is not to be simple secularism, then the alternative must be clearly and enthusiastically made available. And this appears to take us into the tendentious territory of—dare one even say it?—U.U. proselytizing! We have, as a denomination, already cautiously stuck our toe into that forbidding pool to check the waters: we have tried an advertising campaign in Kansas City; we are experimenting with creating a large U.U. congregation from scratch in Texas; and we have launched a Partnership for Growth program that seeks to transform mid-sized U.U. churches into significantly larger congregations. But these steps are indeed tentative. Whether our attempts at making the Unitarian Universalist message more widely available remain tentative or are, instead, taken up on a much larger scale, may make the difference between keeping the re-enchantment of the world a private little U.U. affair, or releasing the mysterious winds of re-enchantment so that they may blow through the wider culture.

Notes for Chapter Six

[1]   A crucially important exception is Germany's preeminent philosopher of the present day, Jürgen Habermas, who attempts to save what he regards as the best parts of the Enlightenment. His voice has probably been the most significant one raised against many of the tenets of postmodern theory. Habermas' notion of reason and truth is built around the idea of free communication among persons, what he calls a theory of "communicative action." Among his concerns are to hold onto a form of reason that can serve as a launching pad for progressive political action.

Printed in the United States
33187LVS00002B/1

9 781413 466911